# A Literary Satellite

# A LITERARY SATELLITE

## *Czechoslovak-Russian Literary Relations*

Milada Součková

The University of Chicago Press
Chicago and London

*Standard Book Number: 226-76840-6*
*Library of Congress Catalog Card Number: 79-99772*

*The University of Chicago Press, Chicago 60637*
*The University of Chicago Press, Ltd., London*


*Published 1970*

*Printed in the United States of America*

# CONTENTS

# PREFACE

In 1945, at the end of World War II, a Western observer might have been surprised by the enthusiasm with which the Czech population greeted the Russian army. True, not all feelings were present on the Prague streets at that historic moment; however, within those limitations, the launching of Czechoslovakia into the Russian orbit in 1945 and the successful completion of this mission in 1948 were welcomed by a substantial segment of the nation. The intellectuals, writers, and poets were by no means a negligible part of it.

To comprehend this situation one must go back as far as the Czech literary renaissance (1774–1859), for since that time Russia has been looked upon as a great Slavic power with the potential to support Czech and Slovak national aspirations. The following chapters inquire into the literary aspects of this Czech-Russian relationship in which the Czechs were first an active agent and only later assumed a passive role. Although chronology is respected, this account nevertheless swings between the present and the past in order to elucidate both the contemporary situation and its history. The study focuses on the "pro-Russian" sentiment and its literary traditions and investigates its most characteristic gropings as they appear in various authors who were in direct contact with Russia.

The First World War, from which the Czechs and Slovaks emerged as a "model" democratic state, put an end to Russophile idealism and brought forth the new, matter-of-fact bolshevik orientation of many writers, among whom the best known is the author of *The Good Soldier Schweik*. Devětsil, the avant-garde group of the early twenties and its foremost personalities were more or less committed to the socialist-communist cause. The prominent author of this postwar generation, Karel Čapek, wrote the manifesto *Why I Am Not a Communist;* but he too pronounced himself in favor of the Stalinist constitution and in the last months of his life was acclaimed by the Russians as a fighter against fascism.

Under Stalinist rule, the doctrine of socialist realism was enforced and its practice supervised among Czechs. In exchange, Czechoslovak literature was favored by Russian scholars and translators. Russo-Czechoslovak relations reached their peak: Czechoslovak scholarship styled itself on the Russian model, using its vocabulary and concepts. The most conspicuous instance of this total merger between the Czech and Russian literary disciplines is *Dějiny českê literatury* [History of Czech literature], the closest imaginable counterpart of the Russian work dealing with the same subject. The Czech classics, J. K. Tyl and A. Jirásek, have been selected as cases typical of the Marxist critical approach to the literary past.

The Russian "thaw," followed by the Czechoslovak destalinization of the sixties, brought a kind of détente—at first shy, but more outspoken and bolder each year. The Czechoslovak intellectual-writer opened an examination of his and society's conscience. Bored and tired of the socialist-realist blueprint, he plunged with relief into the reality of his and other people's lives. And whether intended or not, he found himself involved as a consequence of his cry for personal and public integrity.

The events of August 1968 happened after the completion of this book. They do not necessitate its revision but, on the contrary, add support for its main thesis: the effects of the ideological relationship between Czechoslovak literature and Russia. In a way, however, those events gave it a touch of finality. For with them died whatever was left of nineteenth-century Panslavism and the impact it had had on the Czech and Slovak mind for nearly a century and a half. The main attraction of this orientation was the belief that the powerful czarist, and later Communist, Russia would support and defend the Czech and Slovak national aspirations. And it was precisely this belief which suffered a mortal blow by the 1968 occupation of Czechoslovakia. By this act the political reality of a powerful Slavic nation protecting the interests of its smaller brothers became a myth which the Czech nation rejected in anger, sorrow, and desperation. To bring the Czech and Slovak men to reason, the Russian overseers dispose themselves of efficient means. Yet they will be unable to force upon the Czechoslovak nation free consent to the loss of national sovereignty. The atheistic Czechs never tired of recalling Jan Hus, burnt at the stake because of his inflexibility in matters of religious freedom. Centuries have passed and the image of a Czech executed for his dissent with powerful rulers still remains vivid.

One cannot even guess what course the development of Czech intellectual history will next take. For the time being the young Czech refuses to yield to the idea that Czechoslovakia should look for protection either to the West, as in 1918, or to the East, as in 1945. In other words, he does not wish his national existence impeded by the stronger partner of an alliance. In the present situation such a view seems to be a mere utopia, but perhaps it is only so in 1969.

# 1
# IT BEGINS WITH AN IDEA

THE IDEA which will be discussed in the forthcoming pages is part of a well-known aspect of nineteenth-century intellectual history—Panslavism. *Webster's Dictionary* describes it as a "political and cultural movement originally emphasizing the cultural ties between the Slavic peoples but later associated chiefly with the Russian expansionist policies." But as in so many definitions this one too leaves something to be desired. Those "cultural ties between the Slavic people" were an expression of the national aspirations of smaller Slavic nations, rather than of the expansionist policy of Russia explicit in the Russian Slavophilism. *Webster's* definition also omitted the major role which language played in the Panslavic movement. Today with the Slavophil concept victorious and the expansionist policies of Russia flourishing, the Panslavic idea is mostly history, but not entirely.

The author of the idea, the man who gave it the impetus necessary to influence the intellectuals of his time, was J. G. Herder. This father of the Romantic concept of Slavdom admired Russia. For him it was evident that Russia had a great future. He conceived Europe as a cultural unity and wrote that "not one of the

European nations has attained its cultural standards in isolation."[1] He even put this idea into literary practice when he adapted the Czech myth about Libuše for his poem *Die Fürstentafel* and quoted as his source the Czech chronicle by Hájek. Herder wrote with Romantic enthusiasm about the national folk song and literary monuments of the medieval past; yet by praising the beauty of the German language and the strength of his nation, he was not excluding other Europeans and even less the Slavs. It was he who drew the map of a territory reaching from the Adriatic Sea to the Baltic and from the Russian Don to the Czech Labe (Elbe). It was he who prophesied that the Ukraine would be a new Greece.

The Czechs were versed in Herder's ideas. Fortunát Durych (1735–1802), the founder of Czech Slavistics, was a student of Herder's. Dobrovský and Jungmann both published Herder's passage about the future greatness of Slavs. The Slovak poet Kollár studied Herder, as did the historian Palacký. Every Czech intellectual of the Czech literary renaissance knew Herder's Slavic geography by heart. A member of a relatively small and politically oppressed nationality under the rule of the Austrian Empire, a Czech or Slovak had every reason to look with wishful thoughts on the ethnographic map of the Slavs.

This is not the place to cite all the Czech poets and writers whose work reflects Herder's vision of the brilliant Slavic future. One poet, however, must be introduced, since in him, and in him par excellence, the Panslavic idea acquired its most articulate form. He was the Slovak Protestant priest Jan Kollár (1793–1852). He wrote in Czech because in his time the division between literary Czech and Slovak existed principally in theory.[2] Should poets be divided following their temperaments, Kollár would belong to the category of sanguine romantics. His Panslavic bias

1. J. G. Herder, *Sämtliche Werke*, 17 vols. (Tübingen, 1807) 6:47.

2. After some discussions and controversies, literary Slovak was codified in 1851; the writer principally associated with this event is L'udevít Štúr (1815–56).

was often irritating, his tone of righteousness displeasing; yet he was a great poet. Like the majority of his Slovak intellectual contemporaries, he studied in Jena, where he spent two years at the time when it was celebrating the three hundredth anniversary of Luther's death. He listened to the lectures of the theologian Gabler, the historian Luden, the philosopher Fries, and the scientist Oken. He met the young Wieland[3] and in Weimar spoke with Goethe. The lectures of Heinrich Luden were particularly popular and for extracurricular reasons: they offered to students lessons in German patriotism. Luden talked to them about the future greatness of Germany; he warned them against cosmopolitanism and pictured to them a German republic, a creation of the true German spirit. Luden spoke against any form of slavery and oppression and gave, as a historical example of the German genius, the German Reformation.[4]

Kollár listened with open ears and heart, and what he heard he automatically transposed into a Czech-Slovak context. He was a true Romantic in his sentiment and ideas, yet very masculine in their formulation. Even his youthful romantic love ended as an idea: his one beloved Mína transcended into an allegory following the example of Dante's Beatrice. Kollár's sonnets and epigrams, his Sunday homilies, his travelogues, or his famous blueprint for the Slavic cultural exchange—all these were written with intellectual gusto. His love for the Russian nation was such that he was offended when a newspaper reported the drunkenness of Russian soldiers. His Panslavism, however, was not limited to petty notions; for him a Slav was distinguished by his Slavic idiom, by his respect for freedom and for human dignity. It was for this attitude that T. G. Masaryk admired Kollár. Inspired by Herder, Kollár saw the Slavic territory reaching from Athos to Triglav, from Prague to Moscow, and gradually he styled himself as a prophet of the Slavs' future greatness,

3. The son of Christoph Martin Wieland (1733–1813).

4. Heinrich Luden, *Über das Studium der vaterländischen Geschichte* (Gotha, 1828).

standing with one foot on Tatra and the other on the Urals.[5] The rhetorical question of one of Kollár's sonnets—"Co z nás Slávů bude za sto roků" (What shall we Slavs be in a hundred years?)[6]—received a fairly clear answer some hundred and fifty years later.

The prophet Kollár was often didactic and sectarian; yet he knew how to refresh his reader with a well-written line of poetry. When writing in prose, he was bound to be much more pedestrian and would overwrite his ideas into absurd dimensions. For example, in his Italian travelogue (to his distress he was never able to go to Russia), he found that Italy was the oldest Slavic country and its Etruscans originally Slavic people. In the field of etymology particularly, he built for himself a notorious reputation. The criticism of his more sober contemporaries like Jungmann, Šafařík, or Palacký did not disturb this stubborn Romantic, who enjoyed the sunrise over Venice as "only a Slav might." In his Budapest parish he continued to preach freedom, tolerance, and love for one's native language and to praise the Herderian Slavic virtues of hard work and innocent merriment. Without Kollár, however, the Czech Panslavic idea would have stalemated, and without his easy-to-memorize stanzas it would hardly have influenced the Czech nation so profoundly.

In his *Über die literarische Wechselseitigkeit zwischen verschiedenen Stämmen und Mundarten der slavischen Nation* (1837), Kollár drew a parallel between "Graecia magna" with its Ionic, Aeolic, Doric, and Attic dialects and "Slavia magna" with its Russian, Polish, Czech, Slovak, Bulgarian, and Serbo-Croatian languages. He asked for the establishment of Slavic bookstores in all Slavic capitals, including Vienna. He urged an exchange of books between universities and learned societies and the publication of a magazine in Slavic languages; he insisted on the compilation of an all-Slavic dictionary, on one single Slavic orthography, and on the elimination of all foreign words from the lan-

5. Jan Kollár, *Slávy dcera*, canto 3 ("Dunaj"), sonnet 375.
6. Ibid., sonnet 376.

guage. He pleaded for the well-organized and systematic collecting of Slavic folk songs, for public and private Slavic libraries, for the foundation of Slavic university chairs. Some of his proposals aroused interest in Germany and Russia, the countries occupied with the idea of cultural expansion and national self-assertion. In Russia especially, Kollár's ideas found responsive minds. The historian M. P. Pogodin translated the *Wechselseitigkeit* a year after its first publication, and it appeared in the journal *Otechestvennye zapiski* in 1840. Young Russians from the universities of Moscow, Petersburg, Kharkov, and Kazan went abroad to study Slavic languages, literatures, archeology, and ethnography. Kollár's proposal to found Slavic libraries and to collect Slavic folk songs was also taken into consideration, as well as his all-Slavic magazine.

At that time when the Western world had but a scanty knowledge of the Slavic nations, the Russians, Germans, and Czechs were well informed about Slavic studies in their respective countries. This interest was centered in the field of Slavic linguistics and early Slavic history. The ideological infringement could hardly be avoided and there was no desire to do so. The Russians knew very well the work of Josef Dobrovský (1753–1829), the student of Fortunát Durych. When in 1813 the Napoleonic Wars brought the Russians to Prague, Dobrovský, responding to the general interest in Russian language, wrote the handbook *Verzeichnis der russischen Wörter und Redensarten* (1813).[7] The Napoleonic Wars, the Vienna Congress, and the Russian army in Bohemia and Slovakia made real the previously vague contours of the Russian people.[8] In his memoirs Kollár recalled the Russian cossacks as they were returning home through the Slo-

7. The title continues: *die in gemeinen Leben am haüfigsten vorkommen als Hilfsmittel um sich Russen leichter verständlich zu machen*. This handbook was a sequel to *Neues Hilfsmittel die russische Sprache leichter zu verstehen, vorzüglich für Böhmen zum Teile auch für Deutsche, selbst für Russen die sich den Böhmen verständlich machen* (1799).

8. The Russian army was in Bohemia during the years 1798–1800 under the command of Suvorov, in 1805 under Kutuzov, and again in 1813 and 1815.

vak towns of Turce and Mošov. He reported that the Slovaks liked the Russian songs and the Russian language, some of which they were able to understand. Kollár saw Czar Alexander I and later dedicated to him sonnet 39 in the fourth canto of his *Slávy dcera.*[9]

Panslavic sentiments had their counterpart in scholarly exchange. In 1822 Dobrovský published the first grammar of Church Slavonic—*Institutiones linguae slavicae dialecti veteris.* A member of the Russian Academy, he was in correspondence with the Russians A. S. Shishkov and N. P. Rumiantsev. The latter, knowing Dobrovský's interest in the evangile *Ostromir*, had a facsimile made and sent it with his compliments to the Czech scholar. Dobrovský reciprocated with a copy of his Church Slavonic grammar. This was Kollár's *Wechselseitigkeit* in practice. An even more intimate relationship existed between the Russian scholars and the Slovak P. J. Šafařík, who corresponded with men of the Rumiantsev circle like Koeppen, Pogodin, Bodianskii, and Sreznievskii.[10] In 1836, Šafařík wrote to Koeppen: "Sie [the Russian Academy] ist die einzige hohe Anstalt für das Slawische in ganz Europa, und vieler Augen sind auf sie gerichtet wie der Gläubige nach Mekka."[11] In a letter to Šafařík announcing that he had been named an honorary member of the Imperial Public Library, M. K. Korff congratulated him on his scholarly achievements: "in Gebiete der slavischen Geschichte und Philologie die so viel zur Verherrlichung des slavischen Namens beigetragen hat."[12]

The most colorful personality among the Russians interested

9. It is impossible to render in English the pun on *Slávy* ("glory," "Slavonic"); roughly the title might be "Daughter of glory, of Slavdom."

10. V. A. Frantsev, ed., *Korrespondence Pavla Josefa Šafaříka* (Prague, 1927).

11. Ibid., pt. 1, p. 348. In 1823 Koeppen came to Prague and met with Dobrovský and Hanka; Bodianskii visited the Czech capital in 1837. He subscribed to the periodical *Časopis českého Muzeum*, followed closely Czech publications, and translated articles by Dobrovský and Hanka.

12. Ibid., p. 417.

in Czech Slavistics seems to be A. N. Demidov. He was the owner of platinum mines in the Perm region and a home in Florence, and aimed at "la glorieuse résurrection de la science slave." He addressed Šafařík as "mon cher et respectable Maître," supported his publications financially, and had a translation made of Šafařík's *Starožitnosti slovanskê* under the title *Ethnographie slave*.[13] Could this lively scholarly exchange be compared with the dilettante interest of someone like Sir John Bowring, whose englishing of Czech poetry depended largely on his Czech correspondents? Or can one compare Kollár's magnificent collection of Slovak folk songs—a work done, as he himself put it, "with the left hand" and for his private enjoyment—with the elegant but slightly false *La Guzla* of Mérimée?

Another Czech Slavist who had contacts with the Russians was Václav Hanka, the famous falsifier of medieval Czech manuscripts. Hanka's personality removes him from the group of Russian-oriented Czech scholars and poets of the period. It is not merely his masterful literary forgery but the person behind it who attracts our attention. As far as the Russians were concerned, he was as much a Slavophil as any of his literary colleagues. In 1852, he wrote to the Slovak A. Radlinský that he had in print the evangile *Ostromir*, the publication of which—Hanka hoped—would benefit all Slavs.[14] Yet Hanka knew how to keep aloof from the Panslavic commitment which left scars on the lives of many a Czech. He was the owner of a ring given to him by Czar Alexander I for his translation of the *Igor Tale* (1821), he had received the Russian Order of Saint Anna, and he was never molested by the Austrian police, as his confreres often were.

The Czech scholars and literati took care that the Czech reading public should be acquainted with Russian literature both ancient and modern. The first anthology of modern Czech po-

13. The Russian translation appeared in two editions, 1837 and 1848.

14. P. Bogatyrev, ed., *Korespondencia V. Hanku s A. Radlinským* (Turčianský Svatý Martin, 1940).

etry[15] contained a translation of a poem by M. M. Kheraskov, and by the middle of the nineteenth century the Czechs could read such authors as Gogol, Krylov, Pushkin, and Lermontov. The most gifted and dedicated translator of Russian poetry was the Russophile L. Čelakovský, a poet in his own right. He brought to the translation his gift of poetry and his enthusiasm for Russia. His *Ohlasy písní ruských* [Echoes of the Russian songs, 1829] is a charming pastiche on the Russian folk epic (*byliny*), and with time it has become a Czech classic. Čelakovský cherished but one great ambition: to live in Russia. He even went to Vienna to seek an audience with Czar Alexander I and to ask for employment in Russia. He was very near the fulfillment of this dream when in 1829 the Russian Academy named him, together with Šafařík and Hanka, as its librarians. Finally, in 1842, instead of going to Russia, Čelakovský went to teach at the University of Breslau. *Ohlasy písní ruských* contained a poem with the title *Velká panychida* [The great feast for the dead], which commemorated the burning of Moscow in 1812. On the strength of this tradition another poem was written in 1945, by Vladimir Holan, who used not merely a part of the title—*Panychida*—but also followed the Panslavic messianism of his predecessor; Holan's poem was dedicated to "all brothers who were tortured to death and fell in the second terrible war against the Slavs in 1938–1945." Čelakovský's or Kollár's "Slavophil" verse never disappeared from the Czech and Slovak schoolbooks; the Czech mind was well prepared by its classics for the ideological and political alliance with Russia.

One has to think of Kollár's *Wechselseitigkeit* when one glances at the 1942 project of the Rusian Academy. Its Slavic Commission published a design for a multilateral research program which would study (*a*) the role of the Slavs in world history and culture, (*b*) the role of Russians and Russian culture in the history of the Slavs, (*c*) ethnogenesis of Slavic nations, (*d*) past and present cultural relations between the Slavic nations on the basis of

15. *Almanachy Antonína Jaroslava Puchmajera*, 4 vols. (1769–1820), vol. 1.

their history, folklore, language, literature, archeology, etc., (*e*) history of the struggle of the Slavic nations for their liberation and independence, and (*f*) origins and development of the concept of state and law by the Slavic nations.[16] Thus after more than a century, the great idea of the Czech literary renaissance manifested its longevity; it never lost its hold on the minds of Czech and Slovak intellectuals, who as writers kept it alive in the consciousness of their nation.

16. *Slavica v české řeči*, Slovanský ústav, Studie a prameny, vol. 3, sekce jazyka a literatury (Prague, 1955) 1:5. A related problem, differently formulated and more limited, had been proposed for study in 1791 when the ambassador of Catherine II, P. N. Rumiantsev, asked Dobrovský for comprehensive information about past Czech-Russian relations. V. A. Frantsev, *Ocherki po istorii cheshskovo vozrozhdeniia* (Warsaw, 1903), p. 23.

# 2
# THEY TRAVELED TO RUSSIA

DURING the nineteenth century a trip to Russia often meant more than any other travel experience to a Czech. For him, Russia had been surrounded by an ideological halo since the time of the Czech literary renaissance.

Karel Havlíček (1821–56), the sharp-witted journalist and satirist, to whom his contemporaries listened with respect and posterity with awe, went to Russia in the fall of 1842 and stayed a year and a half. Šafařík, whose name opened doors in the society of Russian Slavists, recommended him as a tutor to M. P. Pogodin, who ceded him to the family Shevyrev. Havlíček, like many of his fellow university students, dreamed about "the great Slavic nation" and the Slavic brotherhood. He brought to Moscow the zest to learn all about his "beloved Russia."[1] In Moscow he had the opportunity to meet the men of the Slavophil circle, which included both Pogodin and Shevyrev. Some of their literary views might have reminded him of Kollár's, whose dislike for Byron paralleled closely the Slavophil criticism of Ler-

1. B. Vavroušek-Slavětínský, *Památník Karla Havlíčka* (Prague, 1921), pp. 109, 113.

montov and Pushkin. Shevyrev admired Gogol, and his literary taste was probably the source of Havlíček's interest in this writer. Havlíček was present at the Moscow University examination in the Czech language presided over by Professor J. M. Bodianskii. He was enchanted (*okouzlen*) by the reference to Šafařík's work as well as by the knowledge of Czech displayed by the students, and wrote an enthusiastic report about this event to the magazine *Květy* in 1843. The enchantment however was short lived. In Havlíček's letter to Zap we hear a new sober note: "The Russians know how to use the idea of Slavic unity better than we do; it [Panslavism] was our idea, we invented it, but we were left in the lurch [*sušíme hubu*[2]]." In another letter to Zap, the disillusionment continued: "I learned Russian, I know Moscow, and I can only say that whoever wishes well to Czechs, let him pay their travel expenses to the Russian capital."[3]

With his usual perspicacity Havlíček differentiated between a Slavophil and a Panslav. Slavophils aimed at a great Slavic empire with Russia as its leader, whereas Panslavs worked for a federalist Slavic union, *pari inter pares*. Havlíček, who at home fought for democratic freedom, found Russia a tremendous obstacle to political progress. "The Russians our Slavic brothers and the Russian government are two different things."[4] With his competent pen Havlíček described to the Czechs colorful scenes from Russian life—the churches and the *kupechestvo* (merchants)—but he was unable to accept the autocratic regime as he observed it in Russian life and institutions. Soon the admiration changed into satire. The epigram *Obiavlenie* [Announcement] is a choice attack on the Czech Panslavic idea:

2. As was his habit, Havlíček used a racy colloquial expression, difficult to render in English and here only approximated by "left in the lurch."

3. Ibid. p. 115.

4. Ivan Pfaff and Vladimír Závodský, eds. *Tradice česko-ruských vztahů v dějinách* (Prague, 1957), p. 121.

*V Evropě se ztratil*
*před dvěmy sty lety český král*
*žádá se uctivě*
*by ho, kdo ho najde odevzdal*
*v Petěrburku Mikuláši cáru*
*dá mu za to bečku kaviáru.*

("Two hundred years ago in Europe, a Czech king was lost; whoever finds him is requested politely to deposit him in Petersburg with Czar Nicholas; the reward is a barrel of caviar.")

Havlíček's warning that the Russians were reaping the benefits of the Panslavic idea passed and continued to pass unnoticed. When Havlíček was read in modern editions and no longer secretly in confiscated or handwritten copies, his criticism of Russia was understood as an attack on its autocratic system. He saw clearly that the idea of a great Slavic brotherhood contained the danger of a stronger partner. His immensely popular *Křest sv. Vladimíra* [The christening of Saint Vladimir], written during 1849–54 but not published until 1876, was enjoyed as an attack on Austria; the fact that the original model was Russia passed without stirring any particular attention.

The largest and most important group of Czechs ever to visit Russia during the nineteenth century were the travelers to the Moscow Ethnographic Exhibition in 1867. This journey was called "pouť Čechů do Moskvy" (the Czech pilgrimage to Moscow), and as such it remained known in Czech history. It made history indeed. The diplomats of both Russia and Austria were alerted. The Russian secretary of interior asked for instructions on the reception of Czechs. The Austrian ambassador reported from Petersburg, where the Czechs stopped on their way to Moscow: "Ces messieurs sont pour le moment les lions de St. Petersburg." Who were those gentlemen lionized in the Russian capital? The most important among them were undoubtedly F. Palacký and F. Rieger, although there were others able to impress their hosts: Dr. Julius Grégr, Dr. Brauner, Dr. Tomáš Černý. The poet and ethnographer K. J. Erben and the artist Q. Manes added diversity to the political group. The Czechs were given an audience by the czar, they were dined and wined by the secretary of education, Zimnii Sad was illuminated in their honor, and not unlike the official visitors of today, they saw a Russian ballet and an opera. "On les traîne de fête en fête et dans les rues on court après leurs voitures pour voir 'les Slavs,' " continued the report of the Austrian diplomat.[5]

In Moscow crowds awaited their arrival, and the mayor of the city gave a dinner in their honor. A minor member of the Czech delegation, the son-in-law of the writer and police informer Karel Sabina, wrote letters to his father-in-law, who sold them to the Austrian police. The son-in-law, blissfully unaware of the fate of his epistles, was sending enthusiastic reports which today represent a first-class source of information. The ethnographic exhibition sponsored by the Archduke Constantin was only a secondary issue of the "pilgrimage." This was understood by all the parties involved. No one could have missed the politico-ideological impact of the Czech visit, neither the Austrian Secretary of State Beust nor any of the Czech patriots. They all agreed that the main goal of the journey was nothing more nor less than a manifestation of the great Slavic unity. The czar and his conservative entourage were cautious; they realized that a union of Slavic nations might give Russia a key position among the Slavs, but on the other hand, they identified Panslavism with progressive ideas, democracy, and socialism. General Shuvalov defined Panslavism (differently from *Webster's*) as "démembrement de la vieille Russie authoritative que nous tenons à conserver."[6] Moreover, the Russians had some misgivings about the Poles and about the Roman Catholicism of the Western Slavs. In spite of these problems the Czech visit ended successfully. The Austrian ambassador tried to minimize the significance of the "soi-disant nationalité slave unitaire." Nevertheless, the Moscow pilgrimage had to be accepted as an important event; "the Austrian

5. Karel Kazbunda, *Pouť Čechů do Moskvy* (Prague, 1924), pp. 54–71. Cf. Milan Prelog, *Pouť Slovanů do Moskvy roku 1867* (Prague, 1931).

6. Kazbunda, *Pouť Čechů do Moskvy*, p. 49.

government will have to realize that it cannot treat the Czechs as a negligible entity,"[7] wrote Sabina's son-in-law.

The politico-cultural result was even more tangible. At home the Czech press made much of the occasion, and Czech enthusiasm for Russia seemed overpowering. The Vienna police reported: "wenn diese Herren [Czechs] davon [about the Moscow journey] erzählen, so kommen sie in eine Extase, es ist nicht zu glauben, wie die Russen auf unsere Landsleute eingewirkt haben."[8] Discounting the different emotions, the result of the Moscow pilgrimage was evident. The Austrian government had to take into account the Czech unwillingness to be second to Germans and Hungarians of the monarchy (the dualist system was introduced the year preceding the Moscow journey) and had to accept the Czech national determination to make itself heard within and outside Austrian territory. It had to consider as reality what some decades before had been only a literary dream and what the Bach regime thought it could eradicate—Czech nationalism and its political potential. The Czechs had their own doubts, of course. Palacký, Rieger, and Grégr were men experienced in politics and would not themselves be carried away by mere enthusiasm; yet they too were ready to make the most of their Moscow journey.

One of the reporters who wrote about the "Moscow pilgrimage" for the daily *Národní listy* was Servác Heller (1845–1922). He was reporting from "inside Russia," since he was a tutor in a Moscow family and familiar with the Russian way of life. Encouraged by the Czech interest in Russia, he published *Život na Rusi* [Inside Russia, 1868], a travelogue which, though it had none of Havlíček's original aperçu, nevertheless offered first-hand information. His travels included distant parts of the Russian Empire. Overwhelmed by its dimensions, he saw it as the most powerful state in the world with a great future ahead to which all Slavs might look with hopeful expectations. He con-

7. Ibid., p. 130 (my translation).

8. Ibid., p. 71.

ceded that Russia was an autocratic state but believed that the Russian absolutism would be liberalized with time.[9] Many of the Czech subscribers of *Národní listy*, shared Heller's views.

The Czech writers who visited Russia during the Czech liberal era, and whose travels have a counterpart in their literary work, were Julius Zeyer (1841–1901) and more particularly Svatopluk (Sv.) Čech (1846–1908). Julius Zeyer is an author underestimated in Marxist literary history, whether Russian or Czech. This is understandable since his social background, his poetry, and his fiction do not yield to any positive Marxist interpretation. Zeyer went to Russia four times—he was a restless traveler—first in 1873 and for the last time in 1899. His Russian experience left a distinct but not a deep imprint on his work. Stylistically, *Zpěv o pomstě za Igora* [Song of vengeance for Igor, 1882] makes one think of the "Russian echoes" by Čelakovský, and *Ondřej Černyšev* (1875) brings to mind the historical novel as it was later fashioned by Merezhkovskii. Perhaps his most authentic writing about Russia is in the first pages of the story "Alexěj člověk boží" [Aleksei, man of God, 1899], which describe a voyage on the Dnieper and the *kalieka perekhozhii*—a group of itinerant crippled beggars.

Sv. Čech was only twenty-eight when he went to southern Russia. In 1874 he visited Tbilisi, which in his travelogue *Upomínky z Východu* [Memories of the East, 1875] has the old name Tiflis. Sv. Čech traveled by boat, stagecoach, railway, and *telega*. He saw the Caucasus through the eyes of Pushkin and Lermontov, whose *Mtcyri* [The novice] and *Kavkazkii plennik* [The prisoner of the Caucasus], he had read in Czech translation as a student.[10]

In 1874 he did not find the Cherkess people "vse russkomu mechu podvlastno," but he was still able to admire the scenery where the heroes of the great Russian poets lived (in *Ve stínu lípy* [In the shade of the linden], 1879):

9. Servác B. Heller, *Život na Rusi* (Prague, 1868), pp. 1, 240, 253.

10. Sv. Čech, *Druhý květ* (Prague, 1899), pp. 129, 130.

*Pak objevil nám Kavkaz mlhy krovem*
*kamennou hruď zeleně huňatou*
*v zátoky krásné klíně azurověm*
*náručí hor nás objal rozpjatou. . . .*

Sv. Čech blended his travel and literary experience in his narrative poem *Čerkes* [The Cherkess], which is indeed a close parallel to *Kavkazkii plennik.* The most popular echo of his Russian sojourn is chapter 7 of the poem *Ve stínu lípy*, which narrates the romantic story of a Czech exile in the Caucasus. In the tradition of the Czech Panslavs, Sv. Čech regarded the Russian expansion to the east and south as the inevitable consequence of Russian strength. His interest and admiration for Russia was the direct heritage of the Czech literary renaissance and more precisely of Kollár, whose rhetoric and grandiloquence had an influence on his poetry.

"A Czech is born with a love for the Russian people,"[11] wrote the Slavophil Josef Holeček (1853–1929). He arrived in Russia with letters of recommendation to N. A. Popov from the Moscow University and to V. T. Lamanskii from Petersburg University. He knew T. D. Florinskii from Moscow University and A. A. Kotchubinskii from the University of Odessa. Like Havlíček before him, Holeček found out that Russian Panslavism meant the domination of Slavs, Poles, Bulgarians, and Czechs by the Russians and that their liberation from the German-Austrian yoke meant their surrender to Russian leadership.[12] Lamanskii expounded to Holeček an idea only realized over half a century later: the Czechs will have to learn the hard way before they will understand the crux of their situation, namely, that their geographical position between the two giants, Germany and Russia, virtually means their submission either to the latter or the former. Even then Lamanskii spoke about a sort of "Sudetenland" (*uzavřené území*) as a solution for the Czech-German an-

11. Josef Holeček, *Ruskočeské kapitoly* (Prague, 1891), p. 3.

12. Holeček, *Zájezd na Rus* (Prague, 1924), p. 13.

tagonisms.[13] In Holeček's time, the majority of Czechs would have rejected such an idea as foolish; Holeček, however, continued to admire the Russian Slavophils, including their "samoderzhavie," which he interpreted as something different from the absolutist state. There is even a touch of anti-Semitism in his vignette describing the train journey from Tarnopol to the Russian border. His was a rather isolated attitude among the Czechs.

Some Russians regarded Czechs as revolutionaries—in this they were influenced by the Austrian Government; the Russian liberals and intelligentsia, on the contrary, considered them reactionaries. The Slavophils looked down upon them and had more sympathy for the orthodox Slavs. "The Czech image of Russia was one great illusion; yet it served its purpose and made the Czech hopes for the future possible."[14]

The Russian impact on modern Czech culture is expressed best by the writer Vilém Mrštík (1863–1912);[15] indeed, Mrštík might be chosen as the man who best illustrates the Czech interest in nineteenth-century Russian realist fiction. He organized *Ottova Ruská knihovna* (1888), a series of translations from the Russian, and he himself translated from Tolstoy, Chekhov, Turgenev, Gogol, Dostoevsky, and Gorki. His translation of *War and Peace* (1888–90) was the first Czech translation of this novel. In 1896, Mrštík got the assignment from the Prague newspaper *Politik* to report on the fair in Nizhnii Novgorod. His *feuilletons*, written in Czech, were translated into German and heavily censored. Like those who visited Russia before him, Mrštík sought the answer to the question: How much help could the

13. Ibid., p. 22.

14. Antal Stašek, *Vybrané spisy* (Prague, 1961–64), vol. 6, *Ze vzpomínek* (1964), pp. 309, 310. The author, father of Ivan Olbracht, went to Russia as a tutor and was there in 1874; Czechs had a good reputation as tutors, nearly as good as beer brewers and musicians.

15. Mrštík was a keen intellectual and sensitive artist, known mostly for his drama *Maryša* (1899) and his impressionnist novel *Pohádka máje*.

Czechs expect from the Russians in their struggle for independence? In a private letter Mrštík gave a blunt answer: Russian help would amount to an exchange of the Austrian terror for the Russian.[16] Like Havlíček before him, he criticized sharply the Russian autocracy, militarism, bureaucracy, and the expansion to the east.[17] This negative attitude of his was counteracted by his admiration for the Russian writers, poets, and literary critics like N. A. Dobroliubov and Belinskii. These interests and their issues were detached from any Slavic sentiment; they were purely literary. Nevertheless, the popularity of the Russian realist drama and novel among the Czech public, toward which Mrštík had contributed a large share, could not but strengthen the existing pro-Russian feelings. Such feelings brought Tchaikovsky to Prague; he conducted a program of his works and entered in his diary of 1888: "I have become very fond of these good Czechs. And there was a reason for that!!! My goodness! I was showered with honors, which of course were meant not for me but rather for dear Russia."[18]

World War I brought Czech interest in Russia closer. The story of the Czech legionnaires in Russia is known as part of world history. Less well known are its Czech authors. One of them, however, achieved fame—the author of *The Good Soldier Schweik*. The Czech legionnaires lived among the Russians, fought with them and against them, and learned the language. Some of them embraced the orthodox faith and took Russian first names. The politico-ideological conclusions of their experi-

16. Radegast Parolek, "Cesta Viléma Mrštíka do Ruska, 1896," Acta Universitatis Carolinae, Philologica (1960) 2:129–37.

17. Ibid., p. 132.

18. Ip. I. Tchaikovsky, ed., *Dnevniki P. I. Chaikovskovo* (Moscow, 1923), pp. 197–98. In 1900, the group of Russian artists called Peredvizhniki had an exhibition in Prague; their aim—as an association— was popularization of art and they had held exhibitions in Petrograd and other Russian cities. The best known of the group are Repin and Serov. In 1906, K. S. Stanislavskii with his ensemble gave a guest performance of Gorki's *Na dne* (The lower depths) in Prague.

ence were often diametrically opposed. At one extreme was Hašek who started to write the first draft of his *Schweik* in Kiev and later joined the Red Army; at the other was Rudolf Medek (1890–1939), the author of novels[19] describing the formation of the Czechoslovak Legions, the part they played in the Russian civil war, and finally their march from the disintegrating Russian front in the south to Vladivostok, proudly called the "Czech anabasis." There were others like Jaroslav Kratochvíl, whose fictional record of this part of history had a different, "bolshevik" orientation.[20]

The first Czech writer to go to Russia from the new Czechoslovakia was Ivan Olbracht (1882–1952), who traveled illegally via Prague and Berlin to Moscow. The year was 1920, and Olbracht's past included anarchist and socialist activities, professional journalism, and one or two successful books. His reportage from Russia, *Obrazy ze soudobého Ruska* [Pictures from contemporary Russia, 1920], has a title which comes very close to Havlíček's *Obrazy z Ruska* [Pictures from Russia]. Olbracht's aim was not a travelogue about Moscow but its portrayal as the center of the Bolshevik effort to build up a socialist country. Although he conceded that the shops of the Russian capital, once full of luxury, were now poor, Olbracht sneered at those who criticized the low standard of Russian life. He argued that the previous opulence was accessible only to the happy few, while millions were living in dire poverty. He did not try to camouflage the scarcity of commodities; yet he always hastened to add that this was merely a temporary restriction.

Olbracht was not an economist, and his views about the Soviet economy were a repetition of the current Marxist argument. In this respect he had no doubts, and any contradiction had no effect on him. He became irritable when he dealt with the doubts

19. *Velké dny* (1922), *Ostrov v bouři* (1925), *Mohutný sen* (1926), *Anabase* (1927).

20. Jaroslav Kratochvíl, *Prameny* (Prague, 1934); this voluminous novel was started in 1924.

of others about the cultural gains of the October Revolution (see the chapter in *Obrazy* titled "Dopis panu Jaroslavu Kvapilovi" [Letter to Mr. Jaroslav Kvapil]). Only then did his real emotions come into the open. Olbracht met Lenin, who knew his articles published in the Russian press. Through the Czech Communist leader, B. Šmeral, Lenin sent Olbracht a box of matches, because in spite of his trust in the Soviet economy, Olbracht used to complain about the shortage of matches. Although from today's perspective, Olbracht's *Obrazy ze soudobêho Ruska* seems to lack literary qualities, it remains a document in the history of Lenin's Soviet Russia. Only a very few outstanding European writers came into direct contact with Russian reality shortly after the October Revolution and witnessed its first developments. In comparison with those who came after him, Olbracht's tone had a matter-of-fact ring. For him, the socialist state was an achievement which he had expected and in whose final success he believed. The most important implication of his 1920 profession of Marxist faith was his firm conviction that some day, not too distant, Czechoslovakia would also become a socialist state.

Four years after Olbracht's visit to Moscow, Marie Majerová arrived there. Like Olbracht, she was a party member and a party worker. She came as a delegate to the International Congress of Women. The Czech group was led by the Communist B. Šmeral, and the period was that of NEP. Majerová visited factories, listened to workers' speeches, and admired everything she saw. She returned to Russia several times and the account of her travels is recorded in *Vítězný pochod* [The victorious march, 1954], a volume of her collected works. With the exception of the holiday in Sochi, all her visits had a political character. She also came during the apogee of the Stalinist era (1947) and did not spare adulatory comments. They appear less exaggerated when compared, for instance, with similar panegyrics of Aragon. Majerová was enchanted with the Russian South and its nature; yet in comparison with what Sv. Čech wrote long before and

Pujmanová soon after, her travelogue communicates mostly pedestrian observations.

Another early traveler to Soviet Russia was the Slovak writer Petr Jilemnický (1901–49).[21] A staunch Communist, like Olbracht and Majerová, he went to Russia for the first time in 1926. The atmosphere of the October Revolution, which still lingered during Olbracht's visit, was buried, and Lenin was resting in the sumptuous mausoleum. It was the time of "uderniky" (shockworkers). The International watched over the discipline of its intellectuals and eventually gave them refresher courses. Jilemnický studied in Moscow's Gosudarstvennyi Institut Zhurnalistiki (Institute of Journalism). He described his two-year stay in the book *Dva roky v zemi sovětů* [Two years in Soviet Russia, 1931]. Jilemnický's reportage abounds in expressions such as "modrá dělnická blůza" (the blue overalls) or "básník-inženýr" (the poet-engineer) that were in vogue with Communist writers of that period; Aragon too used them profusely. Jilemnický's Russian venture is interesting mainly because of his participation in the Czechoslovak project of Interhelpo in Karakirgizia.

Interhelpo was a settlement of Slovaks and Czechs who left Czechoslovakia with the hope of building for themselves a better existence while helping to build up the Soviet economy. Jilemnický used his documentary material for parts of *Kompas v nás* [Our compass, 1936–37], which portrays the authentic story of hardship and superhuman efforts often marred by the inefficiency of the Soviet authorities. The Czechs succeeded in building a tannery and textile factory and established a prosperous community in a place which before had been desert. They were determined to succeed, not so much because they were such dedicated Communists—as are those in the similarly oriented *Den' vtoroi* [The second day] by Ehrenburg—but because their existence and that of their families depended upon it; the problem was not one of ideology but of survival. Jilemnický himself

21. Others early travelers were the linguist Mathesius, the poets Seifert and Hora, the dramaturgist Honzl, the critic Teige, and the writer Kopta.

had to leave the colony because of his poor health; he went subsequently to the Caucasus, where he taught in the village Krasno-Chekhovka, formerly Pavlovka. Into this predominantly Czech settlement, founded in the 1860s, Jilemnický located his novel *Zuniaci krok* [The resounding step, 1930]. The title reflects the march of socialist revolution in a Caucasian village. The content of the novel is collectivization; its style, socialist realism. It teaches that the happiness of the individual is impossible without the happiness of the collective. The Caucasian hero of the Czech neoromantics was engulfed by the story about the *kolkhoz.*

The Russian journeys of men like Jilemnický or Fučík were part of their party activities. They were taught to use their talent for the Marxist cause; their minds and pens were trained for conformity and conformist interpretations. In comparison with them the foremost Czech poet, Vítězslav Nezval (1902–62), appeared a colorful bird among a flock of sparrows. He came as a delegate to the Congress of Writers in Moscow in 1934. Among those invited were the Americans Theodore Dreiser and Sherwood Anderson. A. A. Zhdanov greeted the assembly and Gorki represented the Russian writers. The central issue of the congress was socialist realism, and the words heard from the platform of the congress were to be repeated in countless variation, in countless publications all over the world. Nezval's travelogue, published a year after his visit to Moscow, has the title *Neviditelná Moskva* [Invisible Moscow]. Nezval tells us that he despises the bourgeois world, that he emancipated himself from the capitalist society, and in the same breath speaks of "přeludy" (hallucinations) and "delirantní interpretace" (delirious interpretations). He wrote about meetings and strikes and recalled the Prague café Metro, where he was a habitué. Some Moscow streets reminded him of Bratislava, and Sverdlovsk Square of Chirico's paintings; Sokolniky, where the delegates of the Moscow pilgrimage were guests in 1867, brought to Nezval's mind the Prague Stromovka and the Bois de Boulogne. It is easy to imagine how much this was savored by his hosts. In

Lenin's mausoleum Nezval was moved by the "beauty of Lenin's face" and thought that, had Maiakovskii seen it an hour before his suicide, he would have changed his mind. Nezval also gave an account of his meeting with Elsa Triolet in the café of the hotel Metropole. For Nezval, Aragon's leaving the surrealists was a regrettable move. He himself came to the congress with the intent of defending surrealism and integrating it with the Marxist ideology. His surrealist dream about Moscow never left him, even while he was sight-seeing or sitting at a session of the congress. He had the courage, or perhaps "innocence," to mention *Les vases communicantes* in his short address at the congress—*Neviditelná Moskva* was dedicated to André Breton. It is not surprising that this part of his speech was left out in its published form. Nezval deplored the omission, since his object was to bring the problem of surrealism before the Russian audience.

Nezval also had the nerve to criticize contemporary Soviet art and architecture. He pointed to the Russian tradition of modern art as it was documented in the Tretiakov Gallery and suggested that the young Russian artists were secretly devoted to modern art. Nezval's renown, the undisputed value of his poetry, and perhaps also his reputation as an "enfant terrible," made it possible for him to get off scot-free with his performance in 1934. His close friend Karel Teige and the Slovak poet Laco Novomeský, both present at the congress, were later to expiate for similar views. At the time of the congress, however, the personal dangers of literary opposition to the party line were still latent. Nezval shed a tear in the Park of Culture and Rest, and in Zelenyi Teatr was moved as never before by the overture to *Egmont.* He chatted with Pasternak, the only Russian poet who used the word "love" with him. Nezval expounded to him Breton's *Les vases communicantes;* Pasternak smiled and said: "I intend to write a book in prose [he must have had in mind *Doctor Zhivago*] . . . I wish to express by it how difficult it [the period following the October Revolution] was for me. . . . My book will have to portray it with directness and simplicity."[22] We may imagine the sad and mature smile with which the Russian poet listened to his Czech colleague, and we may guess that this was one of the rare moments when the author of *Doctor Zhivago* spoke about his novel to someone from the West who was his equal. What Pasternak may have thought of Nezval's "surrealist lyricism" is irrelevant; it is important to notice how well Nezval was able to sense what was in Pasternak's mind and what the year 1934 could mean for a poet, whether he was Czech, Russian, or French.

Nezval could be amazingly candid about his erotic emotions in a Moscow trolley car but equally sincere about the Russian theater. He did not like V. V. Vishnievskii's *Optimisticheskaia tragediia* [An optimistic tragedy, 1933], the model of socialist drama, despite his admiration for Tairov. On the other hand, he was enchanted by the presentation of *La dame aux camélias* in Meierkhold's theater. His surrealist attitude, though not quite in harmony with Moscow reality, did not prevent him from giving an unconditional yes to Soviet Russia. He closed his travelogue with true socialist optimism emphasized by italics: "*Svět bude zachráněn, člověk bude šťasten, poesie se zrodí*" (The world will be saved, man will be happy, and poetry will thrive).

In 1934 Julius Fučík lived in Moscow. He was there on a mission dedicated exclusively to the Communist cause both at home and abroad. He sent his articles about life in Soviet Russia to the Prague Communist paper *Rudé právo*. It was a journalistic routine, but Fučík brought to it his dedication to the Marxist idea. When he was traveling to Kirgizia—he took the same route as Jilemnický—he described the bad roads, which for him were precisely the proof of the good quality of Soviet drivers. He noticed with satisfaction that the road from Frunze to Rybacia would be finished before the planned schedule. Fourteen years had passed since Olbracht had complained about the shortage of matches, and Fučík had to ask his wife to send him cigarettes,

22. Vítězslav Nezval, *Neviditelná Moskva* (Prague, 1935), p. 93.

ink, and writing paper.[23] These are unimportant details, Fučík would tell us. The scope of his talent and mind was not so great as the Communists wish us to think. His *Reportáž psaná na oprátce* [Notes from the gallows], written during his imprisonment and shortly before his execution by the Nazis, survived him and was translated into many languages. It is well written, if one may say that about pieces of paper smuggled out of Pankrác Prison, scribbled upon by a man tortured during his hearings and awaiting death. For both the Czechs and Russians he is the hero of World War II.

Marie Pujmanová (1893–1958) visited Soviet Russia in 1932 for the first time. In July of that year she traveled with a group of workers guided by Intourist. At that time she was not a party member, although after her return from Soviet Russia her relationship with the party tightened. She revisited Russia in 1948 and 1953 as an official representative of the Czechoslovak intellectuals, as a writer whose works were translated into Russian, and whose articles appeared in the Russian press. Her travelogue *Zapsáno tužkou* [Written with a pencil] has pages colored with original observation-images; on the other hand, her intellectual attitudes are often hard to digest. Such is, for instance, her presentation of the religious problem in Russia. She would contrast "the Cross with the tractor,"[24] praise the Russian faith in "ideas," and to this she would add that the Soviet atheistic exhibits were as ordinary as a fire extinguisher. Another time she would associate the Bulgarian Dimitrov with the Czech Jan Hus and dabble in the history of Church Slavonic.[25] Yet her visual impressions of the Moscow churches were truly "written with the pencil" of an artist; also her chapter "Rudý Baedeker" [The red Baedeker] is a refreshing description of Tsarskoe Selo and Petropavlovsk. Pujmanová admired the Russian factories and their

23. Julius Fučík, *Korespondence* (Prague, 1963), p. 206.

24. Marie Pujmanová, *Zapsáno tužkou* (Prague, 1957), p. 83.

25. Václav Černý made similar critical remarks about her *Slovanský deník*. Černý, *Kritický měsíčník* (1948), pp. 97, 98.

technology and commented that, unlike the capitalist concern Schneider-Creusot-Krupp, the management of Rudý Putilov had peaceful aims. She visited Tretiakov Gallery and in contrast to Nezval, who praised the collection for its modern art, Pujmanová spoke of the nineteenth-century realists Vereshchagin and Repin. She saw the Russian ballet perform *Paris in Flames*, a performance at which Stalin was present ten days before his death.

The Czech and Slovak writers who traveled in Russia after World War II were numerous. Marie Glazarová, cultural attaché to the Soviet Union, compiled her notes into *Leningrad* (1950), which was seasoned with frequent accolades to the Russian people and their institutions.[26] T. Svatopluk, author of the novel *Botostroj* (1933) about Baťa's Zlín factory, discussed with his Russian friends its new edition. The artist Trnka, known in the West for his puppet films, guided the actor and writer Werich through the treasures of the Hermitage. The Slovak Peter Karvaš wrote *Leningradské epištoly* [Epistles from Leningrad], which is free of the over-enthusiastic tones of the older generation, although like them he praises the Soviets and their friendship for Czechs and Slovaks. In his sixty-three-page travelogue he stresses the Soviet knowledge of Czechoslovak affairs, both in literature and in economy. The tradition of Panslavism, or better of Slavophilism, still lives albeit in an entirely different world.

26. Glazarová's first book, *Roky v kruhu* (1936), had a rather unusual success and at once placed her among the well-known Czechoslovak writers, an "official" position which she has held ever since. Throughout the years she continued steadfastly her Russian line, until the crisis of summer 1968, at which time with another conformist author, J. Drda, she publicly and solemnly revoked her former loyalties (*Rudé právo*, 27 August 1968).

# 3
# THE RED COMMISSAR

*The Good Soldier Schweik* by Jaroslav Hašek enjoys a world renown in which neither literary criticism nor literary propaganda have played a substantial part. International fame came to its author posthumously and as if against all literary odds. At home, immediately after its publication, *Schweik* was widely appreciated by Czech readers; it was only later that Schweik's popularity made him a controversial figure in Czech intellectual history and that, instead of being a jester, he was presented as a speaker in the dialogue of ideas.

The very first critical review pronounced *Schweik* to be an antimilitarist novel. The author of the article was Ivan Olbracht, who stressed the antiwar message of *Schweik* and the originality of its hero, whom he defined as a "clever idiot," a "genius-idiot." He also called Schweik "český Honza,"[1] referring to a popular figure of Czech folklore. Honza overcomes the hero's trials not by heroic daring and shrewdness but by a simpleton's directness, which some might define as stupidity. Olbracht was also the first to align Schweik with literary figures such as Oblomov, Faust,

1. See Emanuel Frynta, *Hašek the Creator of Schweik* (Prague 1965), p. 29.

Don Quixote, and even Hamlet. Olbracht's review appeared in the Communist daily *Rudé právo* in 1921; it was and continues to be cited by both Russian and Czech critics. In reading those few pages reprinted in the recent edition of Olbracht's works,[2] one gets the impression of *déjà lu*, because they were quoted in nearly every monograph or essay about Hašek. *The Good Soldier Schweik* first appeared in installments. Their sponsor and publisher was Hašek's friend Franta Sauer, who believed in the book's success. His task was not an easy one; a new section of the manuscript could be obtained from Hašek only with the threat that future payments would be withheld. Meanwhile, Olbracht's enthusiastic evaluation of *Schweik*[3] was not shared by all. Karel Čapek, for instance, brushed *Schweik* to the periphery of his literary horizon. This is understandable, since the young Čapek, right or wrong, was occupied with sophisticated problems of art and literature that were incompatible—so it must have seemed to him—with Schweik and his world. Also the avant-garde of the early twenties with its dada and its revolutions had little interest in promoting *Schweik*. The antagonism was mutual: Hašek loathed any intellectual approach to literature and refused to discuss literary problems even with his intimate friends. The short story "Mezi bibliofily" [Among the bibliophiles] illustrates his contempt for literary discussions.

With the great wave of *Schweik*'s popularity, the question arose whether the hero of the novel was worthy to represent the Czech character—for as such he had been recognized. The parties engaged in the discussion included no less distinguished a person than the president of the Czechoslovak Republic. The state protocol forbade his taking part in the polemics, as he might have done in his previous professorial days; yet there were other channels

2. Ivan Olbracht, *O umění a společnosti* (Prague, 1956), pp. 178–81. The review first appeared in *Rudé právo*, 15 December 1921.

3. Olbracht's enthusiasm might also be explained by the affinity which he must have felt between *Schweik* and his own early short stories like "O lásce k monarchii" (1910) or "Kariera Eduarda Žáka" (1921).

through which he was able to vent his opinion. His verdict on *Schweik* was a straight no. For anyone familiar with T. G. Masaryk's views, this could not have come as a surprise; he must have been shocked by *Schweik*, if only because of its coarse language and obscenities. His protest, however, was based on higher principles: *švejkovina* (to behave like Schweik) was a danger to public morale. The word was already in current use and meant the little man's ways to escape the pressures of society and the state. It was often said that *švejkovina* helped the Czechs to survive the First World War, and the term was applied once again during the German occupation; the Germans understood its meaning and put a ban on the novel.

The main public exponent of the prewar protest against *Schweik* was the poet and writer Viktor Dyk (1877–1931), a man of political commitments and a staunch nationalist. In spite of political antagonisms, Masaryk's and Dyk's protest against *Schweik* was based on the same idea: Schweik was unfit to represent the Czechoslovak national hero. The national ideal (Dyk) and the democratic ideal (Masaryk) must not be dragged into the gutter of irreverent laughter and escapism. Others, perhaps less outraged in their feelings and won by *Schweik*'s humor, thought that the ruthless satire of *Schweik* had a positive message under the Austrian rule, but that it was somehow less desirable in the autonomous democratic Czechoslovakia. Dyk pointed out that *Schweik*'s portrayal of the army entailed views not quite compatible with the dignity of the Czechoslovak army and accused him of nihilism, anarchism, and a disintegrating influence on the national ethics.[4] This was not a merely local political argument. Erwin Piscator, who in 1928 staged *The Good Soldier Schweik* in his proletarian theater, characterized Schweik as a type "ohne gesellschaftlichen Bindungen, der auch in einer Kommunistischen Gesellschaft zersetzend und auflösend wirken

4. Viktor Dyk, "Hrdina Švejk," *Národní listy*, 15 April 1928; Dyk, "O Švejku a deklaraci." Ibid., 26 April 1928.

würde."[5] The defense of *Schweik* was taken up by the young Communist Julius Fučík.[6] He pleaded for Schweik because like many others, and not only Communists, he believed in the literary values of the novel; yet his main motivation for rushing to its rescue must have been his political loyalties. Even if he had taken into consideration the views of Piscator or Dyk about the destructive influence of the novel on society, Fučík would have defended it since he thought of his and Hašek's contemporary Czechoslovakia as a transient form of society and did not wish for its stability as both Masaryk and Dyk did. Moreover, *Schweik* was a satire on the Austrian, not the Czechoslovak army.

In Brecht's *Schweyk in zweiten Weltkriege*, Schweik is an antifascist. It is evident that *švejkovina* might be transposed into almost any society. Not long ago one of Schweik's sayings, *to chce klid* (easy does it), appeared as a slogan in some public places in Czechoslovakia to the great dismay of the officials. Marie Majerová, the senior National Artist, voiced a protest.[7] Although of course the Russians did not and could not identify with Schweik as did the Czechs, they understood the potential danger of *švejkovina*. They explained Schweik's cynical attitude toward the state authorities as aiming at imperialist Austria and its militarism. *Schweik* was to be interpreted historically, that is, as a satire on the Austrian monarchy and its institutions; it exposed imperialist militarism and nothing more. Nevertheless, because of *Schweik*'s ideological ambiguity, the Russians preferred

5. Erwin Piscator, *Das Politische Theater* (Berlin, 1929), p. 202. Max Brod, the propagandist of the Prague literary culture, offered to Piscator his dramatization of *Schweik;* Piscator however, decided to work with Brecht, Gasbarra, and Lania. They settled on a performance with Schweik as the single actor; puppets, marionettes, and a film filled out the other roles. The artist who worked on these aspects of the play was George Grosz. Schweik was played by Max Pallenberg, one of the great actors of this significant period of the German theater. The play was performed from January to April, 1929.

6. Julius Fučík, "Válka se Švejkem," *Rudý večerník*, 21 March 1928; Fučík, "Válka se Švejkem," *Tvorba* 2, 1927–28, no. 9–10, pp. 294–96.

7. Marie Majerová, *Ševcovská polka* (Prague, 1961), p. 134.

Hašek's short stories, especially those which he wrote as a soldier in the Red Army. It is this part of Hašek's life and work that won their wholehearted approval.

Like his Schweik, Hašek was drafted into the Austrian army, stationed in Budějovice, and with his regiment sent to the Eastern front. When Hašek was taken prisoner, or gave himself up to the Russians, his story and Schweik's took different turns. In 1915 the Union of Czech Fighters (*Svaz českých bojovníků*) was formed with centers in Kiev, Moscow, and Petrograd; it was a political and administrative body of Czechoslovak war prisoners who were to form autonomous military units within the framework of the Russian army. As early as August 1914 about seven hundred Kievan Czechs had volunteered to serve in the regular Russian army. By 1917, the Czechoslovak Legions counted forty thousand men.

After the months spent in the prisoner-of-war camp, Hašek landed in Kiev with its large prewar Czech colony and its weekly *Čechoslovan.* During 1916–17, this periodical published his short stories, which had as much success in Kiev as they had previously at home. Hašek was also writing propaganda articles—some of them in verse—in which he ridiculed the Austrian regime and its church. The Russian critic Elanskii,[8] rhetorically asking how it was possible that the czarist censorship released those attacks on the principles of which its own power was built, answered that it was opportune for the Russian imperialists to have the enemy discredited by whatever means at hand. Through his writings Hašek also encouraged Czech and Slovak war prisoners to enlist in the Czechoslovak Legions. *Povídka o záruce* [Security first, 1916] is a satire on a Czech who refuses to join the Legions and lives for his own petty interests.

*The Good Soldier Schweik in Captivity* (1917), also written in Kiev, proves that Schweik had never completely left Hašek's

8. N. P. Elanskii, *Iaroslav Gashek v revoliutsionnoi Rossii* (Moscow, 1960), p. 39.

mind.[9] His life among the Czechoslovak legionnaires must have worked as a catalyst on the formation of his hero. Schweik's social background and its cultural pattern corresponded to that of the soldiers whom Hašek was meeting daily. Like Schweik, they came from the lower middle class, lived in Prague, were drafted into the army and engulfed by World War I. In Kiev, Hašek met men who spoke the same vernacular as his Schweik and who had his particular sense of humor. Indeed he had a living double whose name was Kodl, later known from the yarns of the Russian legionnaires and also from Medek's novels about the Czechoslovak Legions; this man could easily have been taken for a relative of Schweik's or at least for one of the characters in Hašek's future novel. Like other anonymous Czech legionnaires, Schweik despised the Austrian monarchy and its bureaucracy, and poked fun at them. Hašek could not have achieved his satire so forcefully, nor could it have had such a vivid response, had he not been expressing a collective attitude. In Kiev, Hašek wrote "Povídka o obrazu císaře Františka Josefa" [A story about the portrait of Emperor Franz Joseph, 1916]; the subject prefigured the famous episode of Schweik and was also in tune with the current type of jokes about the Austrian emperor. Elanskii cites this short story and comments on it: at that period Hašek shared with other Czechs the idea of liberation of Czechs and Slovaks from the yoke of the Austrian Empire and therefore was able to identify himself with the ideology of the Legions and their leadership. Elanskii states quite correctly that it was the idea of liberation which held together Czechs of different political views, "reactionaries, bourgeois, and liberals as well." In 1917, Hašek sided with the social democrats and Masaryk and Miliukov, because he did not see any possibility of joining a more "progressive group." At that stage of the war, Hašek did not realize the imperialist character of World War I, nor was he advanced enough

9. *Schweik* can be traced as far back as 1911. "Dobrý voják Švejk," *Karikatury*, 1911, no. 21. See also the testimony of Hašek's wife, Jarmila, in Frynta, *Hašek the Creator of Schweik*, p. 106.

to understand the Marxist teachings. In Hašek's defense, Elanskii added that in this period even the Russian masses were under the influence of essers and Mensheviks.[10]

Thus, during the period from May to August 1917, Hašek was still a soldier in the Czechoslovak Legions and took part in the battle of Zborov. He was appalled when the Russian soldiers were "giving up the fight" (*brosili vintovki v zhito*) for he felt that the Czechs might not win their freedom unless Germany was defeated. One has to keep in mind that those historical events of World War I and Hašek's part in them were interpreted by the Russian critics and their literary satellite in strict accordance with the *Istoriia Kommunisticheskoi partii* [The history of the Communist party]. In February 1918, disregarding the armistice, the Germans entered the Ukraine, and the Soviets were organizing the Red Army to resist this invasion. The Czechoslovak Legions, on the other hand, received an order to leave the Ukraine. The directives were issued by Odbočka with Masaryk and Beneš as its top political authorities. The Legions were to march to Vladivostok and from there be transported to the French front and continue to fight on the side of the Allies. The order met with some opposition and murmurs; Hašek was among the dissenters. It was not his first conflict with the policies of the Legions; there had already been considerable friction between him and the leaders. The new decision of Odbočka prompted him to act.[11] When the Czechoslovak Legions mustered for their historical anabasis, Hašek was not among them. At the beginning of March 1918 he left Kiev for Moscow—he was there when Lenin spoke at the Politekhnicheskii Muzei on 12 March 1918. On 17 April 1918 Hašek announced to the *Otdeleniu Natsional'novo Sovieta* his break with the Czechoslovak Legions and joined the Czechoslovak section of RKP, the Russian Communist party.[12]

10. Elanskii, *Iaroslav Gashek v revoliutsionnoi Rossii*, p. 71; *essers* is a term for socialist revolutionaries (henceforth SR).

11. Ibid., p. 107.

12. S. Vostokova, *Iaroslav Gashek* (Moscow, 1964), p. 85.

The first number of *Průkopník* (27 March 1918), the new Communist propaganda periodical, brought out his "historical" article "Proč se jede do Francie?" [Why should we go to France?]. The article made the accusation that the leadership of the Czechoslovak Legions was holding back the truth from the common soldier and that the sole aim of the transport to France was to sever him from the Russian Revolution; it reminded the legionnaires that they were the descendants of the valiant Hussite Taborites, who were the "first European socialist communists."[13] Thus started what Elanskii called *geroicheskii* period—the heroic period of Hašek's life. And it is not an overstatement, at least for those who may read the Russian record of Hašek's involvement in the Russian Revolution in Siberia.[14]

*Idu za Gashekom* [Following Hašek step by step, 1963] by Alexander Dunaevskii, literally follows Hašek's footsteps in the revolutionary Russia of 1919–20. Dunaevskii searched archives, local museums, back numbers of local newspapers and magazines, interviewed people, wrote letters; he went to Samara, Bugulma, Ufa, Cheliabinsk, Omsk, Krasnoiarks, and Irkutsk. In Kuibyshev he found the house where Hašek lived and gives in his book not only the address but also a photograph of Hotel San Remo—an old provincial house, a reminder of another age, where Hašek lived in a room with two windows overlooking the Volga in April 1918. Here the "politicheskii komissar Gashek" of the Fifth Red Army *Politotdel* wrote proclamations like "Tovarishchi soldaty" [Brother soldiers], "Vsem Chekhoslovakam" [To all Czechoslovaks], and "Vojáci revolucionáři" [Revolutionary soldiers]. The Czechoslovak Legions were not far away.[15] After

13. Jaroslav Křížek, *Jaroslav Hašek v revolučním Rusku* (Prague, 1957), p. 177.

14. Stanislav Antonov, *Gashek shagaet po povolzhhiu* (Kazan, 1964); *Iaroslav Gashek v Bashkirii* (Ufa, 1960).

15. In his monograph, Křížek gives an interesting analysis of Hašek's mood of those days (*Jaroslav Hašek's v revolučním Rusku*, pp. 197–99, 201, 202, 215).

the fall of Samara, Hašek was hiding among the Mordovians and Tatars. He assumed the disguise of a "feebleminded son of a German colonist from Turkestan" or gave himself out as the grandson of a certain Dementévna, who worked in a textile factory in Tashkent.[16] Hašek's role of half-idiot was carefully chosen: Turkestan was then in Soviet hands and none of the counterrevolutionaries were able to check on his identity. His Russian accent might have betrayed him, but his German was nearly as good as his Czech. The real danger was to be recognized by "belochekhy." Hašek was rehearsing a part of *Schweik* which he was never to write. It has been suggested that he intended to write *Švejk v Bugulmě* [Schweik in Bugulma]; Elanskii speculated on what the novel would have been like if it reached the world of the Russian Revolution and decided that Schweik would grow out of his negative *švejkovina* and adopt sound communist views.[17] These were idle speculations because the event never took place and because Schweik's character did not allow such change.

The Bolshevik policies regarding the Czechoslovak Legions were handled by Trotsky and Stalin, who negotiated with their leader (Maxa) in Penza. In the meantime, Hašek emerged from hiding and joined the Fifth Red Army as a propaganda writer. He worked for *Nash put'*, a propaganda periodical of the Red Army. There he published his often cited "Iz dnevnika ufimskovo burzhuia" [From the diary of an Ufim bourgeois].[18] Written in Russian, it tells the fears of a Russian merchant who tries to escape the claws of the Revolution. He is a petty man whose only desire is to protect his property. He is not the only mean character of the story; a Czech soldier appears to be his equal. This episodic figure shows how completely Hašek was able to sever himself from his former associates and adopt new ones.

16. Alexander Dunaevskii, *Idu za Gashekom* (Moscow, 1963), pp. 20, 30.

17. Elanskii, *Iaroslav Gashek v revoliutsionnoi Rossii*, p. 136.

18. *Nash put'*, 1919, no. 3; Křížek, *Jaroslav Hašek v revolučním Rusku*, pp. 244–45.

These pages—three in book form and in Czech translation—contain nothing of Hašek's former cynical grip. They might have been written by any experienced writer, perhaps by a second-rate Chekhov. The Russians give an outstanding place to this mediocre story, and so do the Czech critics.

For the *Politotdel* of the Fifth Army, Jaroslav Hašek proved to be a valuable acquisition. "S vostoka na zapad Evropy idet volna revoliutsii. Ona uzhe razbudila sotni millionov liudei a sorvala korony Karla Habsburga i Vilhelma Hohentsollerna . . . [From East to West rolls a great wave of revolution. Already it has stirred millions of people and torn the crown from the heads of Charles Hapsburg and Wilhelm Hohenzollern]" wrote Hašek in *Nash put'*.[19] He was attacking Kolchak, the SR, in short any counterrevolutionary element, *popi* and *dukhovenstvo* (clergy), included—the latter being a current subject of Hašek's satirical repertoire.[20] This *mnogoiazychnyi komissar* (the commissar who knew many languages), as Hašek was called, organized the publication of the first Soviet newspaper in Buriat-Mongolian, wrote for the German *Sturm* and for the Hungarian *Rogam*, spoke before the first plenum of the Krasnoiarsk Soviet, and registered in a course in Chinese, Japanese, and Mongolian at Irkutsk University. At the end of 1919, in Cheliabinsk, Hašek was the head (*nachal'nikom*) of the international group of *Politotdel*, called *Internatsiotdeleniia*. He was working energetically to recruit soldiers of different nationalities—Czech, Slovak, German, Hungarian—to join the Red Army, and also aimed at a more distant goal stressed by Lenin's speech at the congress of the RKP, the indocrination of foreign soldiers.[21] Hašek addressed the soldiers in the name of the international proletariat, hailed the Soviets

19. Elanskii, *Iaroslav Gashek v revoliutsionnoi Rossii*, p. 146; see also Dunaevskii, *Idu za Gashekom*, p. 65.

20. A collection of Hašek's satire on the clergy was published as *Fialový hrom*.

21. Vostokova, *Iaroslav Gashek*, p. 103.

as teachers of the world revolution, and glowed with revolutionary enthusiasm.[22]

He was seriously engaged in his task. The days of his prewar jest on a political party—*Strana mírného pokroku v mezích zákona*—was a matter of the past. Hašek continued to be sober. After World War I, when Olbracht went to Russia and talked with Russians who knew Hašek or heard about him, he was surprised to hear their praise of the commissar who never drank, who was efficient, reliable, a good organizer, a zealous worker, and a courageous soldier.[23] Hašek's activity in the Red Army must have brought him gratification and a sense of purpose which were new to him. All his life he was a radical who hated sincerely the bourgeois world and its orderly way of life. Deep in his heart he was always a nonconformist and never changed in this respect. In Siberia, the situation around him was neither a rigid authoritative regime nor a stabilized society but a dramatically fluctuating adventure of people and places. One of Hašek's Russian friends remarked that he was active in a territory ten times bigger then Czechoslovakia.[24] Ufa, Cheliabinsk, Omsk, Krasnoiarks, and Irkutsk marked the route of the Red Army and the young Communist Hašek. In this part of the world and of his life he was a youthful man in uniform with a *furazhka* (cap) dotted with a red star. So he was seen in a military train whose background was the Siberian steppe.[25] With this image in mind one understands perfectly well why Hašek never laughed about his "red" past. The Czech critic R. Pytlík spoke about this period of Hašek's life with ideological bathos: "In his work for the

22. Elanskii, *Iaroslav Gashek v revoliutsionnoi Rossii*, p. 187.

23. Dunaevskii, *Idu za Gashekom*, pp. 92–97. Compare this portrait with the report of comrade B. Šmeral: "V maličkostech nás obelhává . . ." (He may lie in small things). Jaroslav Křížek, *Jaroslav Hašek v revolučním Rusku*, p. 296.

24. Elanskii, *Iaroslav Gashek v revoliutsionnoi Rossii*, p. 199.

25. Dunaevskii, *Idu za Gashekom*, pp. 87, 88; see also Křížek, *Jaroslav Hašek v revolučním Rusku*, p. 269.

world revolution, Hašek was able to realize his previous concept of the national [Czech] revolution and his idea about the historical role of the masses."[26] Hašek's involvement was not merely a matter of ideas as Pytlík thought, it was a way of life.

In the spring of 1920, the Soviets organized the transfer of Czech and Slovak Communists to Czechoslovakia. Hašek was not pleased when he heard that his turn had come.[27] With a passport in the name Shaidlov he left Moscow for Czechoslovakia in November 1920. It was assumed that he would work among the miners in the coal district Kladno. The great adventure was finished, the horizon shrunk, and its colors grown drab. On his return home, Hašek found that the "vsemirnaia kommuna" (world commune) was not as near as he had announced in his Russian articles and at the meetings in Krasnoiarsk. Instead, he faced the ghost of his own past and the Czechoslovak *beloguardeitsy*, who had his "treason"—his defection from the Legions—still fresh in mind. For the time it was they who were the heroes of the war. Many of them occupied high positions in the new Czechoslovak government. Nevertheless, in spite of hard feelings, no drastic steps were taken against Hašek. His Communist friends could offer him nothing but unattractive work for the party. The only refuge was to start again where he had left off. On the first evening in Prague, Hašek took up drinking. The question of his work in Kladno was not even raised, although Pytlík claims that for Hašek the contact with the Kladno comrades was dangerous and therefore had to be dropped.[28] The Marxist critics put the blame for Hašek's reversion to his bohemian past on the "reactionary" atmosphere which surrounded him after his return.[29] The hostility toward him could not have been "dangerous," or at least could not have lasted long, since

26. Radko Pytlík, *Jaroslav Hašek* (Prague, 1962), p. 82. My translation.

27. Křížek, *Jaroslav Hašek v revolučním Rusku*, pp. 308, 309.

28. Pytlík, *Jaroslav Hašek*, p. 84.

29. Vostokova, *Iaroslav Gashek*, p. 103.

the newspaper *Tribuna*, a new liberal daily, and *České slovo*, the daily of the National Socialists, and finally the government-sponsored *Lidové noviny* all accepted his short stories.[30]

Hašek's notoriety was no asset for the party, which discreetly dissociated itself from his "buffonada." This expression of Elanskii's is a colorful, yet too mild word. Countless anecdotes exist about his gargantuan capacity for revelry; these stories about him alone would fill a volume or two of his collected works. All that remained from Hašek's Russian discipline were his Russian felt boots, his habit of wearing the *rubashka* (shirt), and of course his Russian wife. Hašek used to introduce her as a countess, but both Elanskii and Dunaevskii wrote that she was employed in a printing workshop.[31] She shared Hašek's ignominious life, trying but unable to stop his drinking and his eccentricities. His cynical jokes did not spare anything or anybody; the only subject which his jest never touched was his Bolshevik past and communism.[32] Iaroslav Romanovich was extremely reticent about the Russian period of his life (*chto on delal v Rossii*).[33] In his memoir on Hašek, Longen—who was the first to stage *The Good Soldier Schweik*—wrote that Hašek even refused to discuss the Russian theater with him.[34] Langer, another of Hašek's close companions, recalled his refusal to join any literary discussion, and it was merely his guess that Hašek admired Dostoevsky.[35]

Hašek must have felt that he could not write his masterpiece if he were to remain in Prague. One day, with his "gypsy's" ease he disappeared, leaving his wife and friends without any

30. "Velitelem města Bugulmy," "Slavné doby města Bugulmy," and "Adjutantem města Bugulmy" were published in *Tribuna* in 1921.

31. See also Gustav Janoušek, *Jaroslav Hašek* (Bern, 1966), pp. 212, 213.

32. Olbracht, *O umění a společnosti*, p. 18.

33. Vostokova, *Iaroslav Gashek*, p. 122.

34. E. A. Longen, *Jaroslav Hašek* (Prague, 1928), p. 165.

35. František Langer, *Byli a bylo* (Prague, 1963), p. 14.

clue concerning his whereabouts. He landed in Lipnice, a village where his friend the painter Panuška used to go for his plein air studies. Hašek lived in the village inn, and there his wife joined him. Only during the last months of his life did Hašek settle in a house bought with the first royalties from *Schweik*. The house in Lipnice was his last effort to live as other people did, but it was too late for this experiment. In the Russian prisoners' camp Hašek had contracted typhoid fever, and after his release he never did anything to improve his health. Surprisingly enough, his constant intoxication did not diminish his strength or his unique gifts of memory, wit, and improvisation. He wrote with the same easy carelessness whether he woke up in the studio of his illustrator Lada, in a cheap hotel room, or at the police station. In Lipnice he used to dictate his *Schweik* and some of his stories while he was simultaneously engaged in a conversation with the habitués of a saloon.

Abroad Hašek is known as the author of *Schweik*, and seldom if ever as a writer of short stories. He wrote more than a thousand of them and they represent a practically unexplored part of Hašek's work. There are two reasons for this: general interest has focused on *Schweik*, and the widely scattered story material was collected and published only relatively recently. The Russians translated about one hundred of Hašek's stories; their interest centered on those that show the author as an "uncompromising enemy of the bourgeois world" (V . . . bezkompromissnom otritsani burzhuaznovo mira).[36]

Hašek's caricature of the bourgeois was based on its classical type: the fat, stupid rich man who exploits the thin, oppressed poor with the benediction of those who are in power—the state and the clergy. Hašek's satire was effective because he followed closely the cultural pattern in which he lived. With Flaubertian interest he liked to search the train schedules, handbooks, and

36. Vostokova, *Iaroslav Gashek*, p. 179.

newspaper advertisements. Quickly responding to any stylistic cliché or linguistic peculiarity, he would ridicule a decadent poem as well as the sermon of a priest. The majority of Hašek's stories do not distinguish him from the average professional writer of the humorous genre; if it were not for a linguistic turn of which he was the master, the story might often be only crude literary slapstick. Hašek wrote under different names—he used more than a hundred pseudonyms—and some of his stories could not be identified because they were insignificant and banal. Many of them have a commonplace, vulgar tone which alienated people like Karel Čapek or Arne Novák. The Marxist critics dismissed their approach as purely bourgeois.

Among those hundreds of pages of Hašek's uneven storytelling, an unprejudiced, attentive, and patient reader might come across rare and accomplished literary art. Such is, for example, "Ze staré trestnice v Ilavě" [The old penitentiary in Ilava], written for the popular *Kalendář lidu na obyčejný rok 1915* [The people's almanac for the year 1915]. Karel Čapek and other Czech intellectuals of that period would consider it beneath their dignity to contribute to this kind of publication; furthermore, they would never have been asked to do so. And yet, if there had been a contest for the best Czech short story of the year 1915, Hašek's "Ze staré trestnice v Ilavě" would have been the winner. The story of the old Hungarian-Slovak penitentiary of 1868 has delightful local color with touches of the Hungarian language and is free from Hašek's usual negligence in composition. As early as 1907, Hašek wrote for the periodical *Komuna* a political satire transposed into the Roman Empire—"Příhoda Gaia Antonia Trossula" [An incident of Gaius Antonius Trossulus]; as good as any of Karel Čapek's *Kniha apokryfů* [Apocryphal stories], it was written thirteen years before the first of Čapek's "apocrypha," which appeared in 1920. One of Hašek's best, "O krásné paní a medvědu ze Začaljanské doliny" [The beautiful lady and the bear from Zachaliana dale, 1920], equals if it does not surpass Olbracht's stories set in Carpatho-Russia (written later—1933 and 1937).

"Nad jezerem Blatenským" [Above Lake Balaton],[37] another of Hašek's achievement, has the subtitle "A sketch from Hungary"; it opens with a pastoral setting (unusual for Hašek)—a summer afternoon heavy with storm over the countryside somewhere near Lake Balaton. The owner of an estate sits on his terrace awaiting a visit from the judge. A gypsy was murdered on the grounds of the estate and the crime is under investigation. Shortly before the arrival of the judge, the landlord has an attack of malaria, during which he sees the countryside spread before him in colors changing from yellow to purple. Luckily the malaria chills lessen and pass before the hour of the visit; the landowner sees again his surroundings in familiar colors—the green of the vineyards and meadows, the yellow of the cornfields, the blue of the lake. A servant announces the judge and after an exchange of polite formalities, the two men sit down and the host orders wine to be brought in. It is an exquisite wine, which mellows the mood of the judge, and the following inquest is carried on with Oriental politeness, which warms up after a few glasses of wine. The last serving is even superior to the previous ones, and the judge praises highly its excellence. He is told by his host that it was precisely the theft of twenty bottles of this delicious wine that made him shoot the gypsy. The judge understands perfectly his host's motivations and decides to close the case with the clause that the gypsy was shot by accident. The central motif—justice among men—reminds one, by its subtle presentation, of some outstanding modern writers, perhaps even of Camus. Three of the four stories mentioned here have as their locale Hungary-Slovakia, where the young Hašek roamed and tried to shake off the fetters of family and society.

There is one aspect of Hašek's satire which seems to have been

37. The standard bibliography of Hašek's works (Radko Pytlík and Miroslav Laiske, comps., *Bibliografie Jaroslava Haška* [Prague, 1960]) gives only the dates of the posthumous publication: 1952, 1955.

passed over or nearly unnoticed by his critics. F. X. Šalda makes an honorable exception. About *Schweik* he used such adjectives as "temný, hrozný" (dark and frightening) and found that the novel was "dissonant" without any "harmonious" element.[38] Hašek's humor and satire are not as uninhibited and straightforward as they appear at first. There is a grimace under his laughter, a cruel vision which for a second obscures the "healthy" laughter. Everyone laughs and Hašek is anxious to make this merriment last as long as possible. At times one may observe how he spies on his audience: Do they laugh loud enough? He wants his imaginary reader to be swept away and to forget all about the true face of death, of sex, of suffering, and deprivation; man's helplessness, his social plight, his infantile fears are processed by the mechanism of laughter, and for the moment all pain stops. It is at this moment, which does not occur often, that Hašek himself is agonizingly sober. Both Langer and Longen observed this trait in Hašek's personality.[39]

The Marxist biographers, on the other hand, beautified Hašek's portrait and made him wear a Sunday suit which he never possessed. Vostokova cited A. V. Lunacharskii's remark about the "dobrodushno lukavyi" (good-natured and cunning) humor of *Schweik*,[40] and in order to bring Hašek closer to the ideal of the Communist writer, she wrote about the optimism which he drew from the society of simple people in Lipnice. Her literary sentimentality made her describe Hašek as "nezhnyi muzh" (tender husband)[41]—a very inappropriate characterization indeed. Generally speaking, both the Czechs and the Russians tend to interpret Hašek's scandals as revolt against bourgeois society and to hush up his bohemian life with the solicitude

38. F. X. Šalda, *Šaldův zápisník*, 1928–29, no. 1, pp. 16, 17; see also Václav Menger, *Jaroslav Hašek, zajatec číslo* 294217 (Prague, 1934), p. 63.

39. Langer, *Byli a bylo*, p. 63; Longen, *Jaroslav Hašek*, p. 165.

40. Vostokova, *Iaroslav Gashek*, p. 166.

41. Ibid., p. 100.

of a mother: "The hard work of a bank clerk could not suit the young Hašek."[42] We know only too well that the reason for Hašek's nonconformity was his even then incorrigible, inherited disposition. Vostokova also attributed to Hašek "dobrodushnyi kharacter" (good-natured character), a characteristic contrasting sharply with what we know from other sources.[43] True, Hašek was able to give his second pair of shoes (he liked good shoes) to a vagabond, knowing well that he would sell them to get money for another bout of drinking. He would pay lavishly for the whole company when entertaining. However, he was also capable of downright cruelty, as on the day when he gave some workers pure alcohol to drink and enjoyed their pains. He would refuse carfare to a man with whom he had been carousing all night. Whatever Hašek's virtues were, "human warmth" was not among them, unless one means by that the camaraderie of a jolly companion.

Hašek wrote his own caricature: "Největší spisovatel český Jaroslav Hašek."[44] The funniest part of this self-portrait lies in the fact that it resembles its model. If Hašek was not "the greatest Czech writer" as he claimed in his self-portrait—the phrase itself is a cliché and was used by Hašek as such—he was certainly very close to it in its literal sense. How serious he was when he spoke of himself as a "genius—a hypocrite might say beast [*hovado*]" is really not relevant. In his customary cynical manner, he blunted a possible accusation of conceit by contrasting the "genius" with the "beast." When he thought of himself as the author of *Schweik*, his big word did not seem entirely out of place. He must have been aware of his unique and exceptional talent. He saw the dawn of his fame, though merely the pallor of a dawn. One of his Russian biographers praised him with

42. Ibid., p. 10.

43. Ibid., pp. 159, 137; cf. Pytlík, *Jaroslav Hašek*, p. 123; Elanskii, *Iaroslav Gashek v revoliutsionnoi Rossii*, p. 28; Dunaevskii, *Idu za Gashekom*, p. 88; Longen, *Jaroslav Hašek*, pp. 72, 102.

44. Pytlík and Laiske, *Bibliografie Jaroslava Haška*, no. 1134.

simplicity, not from our literary perspective, but perhaps Hašek would like his toast better than anyone else's: "Proshlo neskol'ko desiatiletii, no i seichas khochetsia aplodirovat' Gasheku" (a few decades have passed and one still feels the urge to applaud Hašek).[45]

45. Dunaevskii, *Idu za Gashekom*, p. 136.

# 4
# AN INTERNATIONAL ASSET

AFTER the author of *The Good Soldier Schweik*, Karel Čapek is the best-known modern Czech writer outside Czechoslovakia: His international reputation began with the success of his play *RUR* (1921), and from then on grew steadily. The stronghold of his renown abroad was England; some of his *Anglické listy* [Letters from England], were translated and published in the *Manchester Guardian* as early as 1924. Even then he was looking beyond the limitations of his native literature. When his first book, *Boží muka* [Wayside cross, 1917], appeared, some of his juvenilia had already been translated into German.[1] After the end of World War I—Čapek was twenty-eight—he had sufficient experience, talent, and ambition to try for a literary career in the new Czechoslovakia. After the completion of his university studies he had some difficulties in finding a position and decided to join the staff of *Národní listy*, one of the foremost newspapers in those days, but he soon left it for *Lidové noviny*, where he enjoyed a unique prestige for the rest of his life. He never seemed

1. *Viktor Dyk, S. K. Neumann, bratří Čapkové* (Prague, 1962), p. 184.

tired of working for the newspaper and a great part of his popularity was earned through journalism.

*RUR* was performed in the United States, England, Japan, and Russia. For the Russians the play had a particular significance. Alexei Tolstoy saw it at the Theater am Kurfürstendamm in Berlin in the winter of 1923, and impressed by it, he wrote *Bunt mashin* [The mutiny of machines]; his play was published in *Zvezda* in 1924 and produced in Leningrad at Leninskii Bolshoi Dramaticheskii Teatr the same year. Tolstoy transposed the conflict between man and technology into the class conflict. In *RUR* the robots revolt against men; in *Bunt mashin* the revolt is directed against the exploitation of labor. Tolstoy added to the cast the figure of the revolutionary Mikhail, agitator and propagandist. Tolstoy's Mikhail identifies himself with the worker and his revolt; Čapek's Domin—the Russians like to connect him with Fabianism[2]—is for a peaceful technological progress (*mirovoi tekhnicheskii progress*). The Russians realized the debt of *Bunt mashin* to *RUR;* for them, however, *Bunt mashin* meant a further step toward socialist ideology. On the other hand, they conceded to *RUR* its primacy in originality and literary importance.

In the Berlin of the twenties, both Tolstoy and Čapek witnessed conditions which aroused their criticism of contemporary society. One might object that neither Tolstoy nor Čapek had to go to Berlin to be aware of the plight of postwar Europe. Yet in a way the Germany of that time bespoke more eloquently the aftermath of World War I than Russia or Czechoslovakia. In Russia the revolutionary turmoil brought sheer misery and tragedy to human lives, although at the same time it gave promise of a brilliant future. To the people of Czechoslovakia, World War I brought to reality a dream and hope cherished for centuries. Ger-

2. Z. G. Mints and O. K. Malevich, *Chapek i A. N. Tolstoi*, Uchenye zapiski Tartuskovo gosudarstvennovo universiteta, no. 65, p. 130.

many, on the other hand, was but defeat. As some of the titles[3] of his first short stories suggest, the young Čapek appears to have been affected by the social conflicts of his time more directly than in his later years, when he could envision Europe as a league of progressive and peace-loving nations; especially when, in economically and politically stabilized Czechoslovakia, he assumed the position of an "official" representative of Czech literature. His *Hovory s T. G. Masarykem* [President Masaryk tells his story, 1928] made him immensely popular. Not only the intellectuals but even the average reader felt that Čapek was *the* modern Czech writer. Čapek was aware of it. "They consider me to be the official representative of Czech literature; as you must know, 'officialdom' in our country is something akin to a curse,"[4] wrote Čapek in one of his letters. Nevertheless, this "officialdom," even if some murmured against it, brought him also a nearly undisputed status of preference. When he visited England, the Czechoslovak Embassy in London exerted itself to make his stay pleasant and profitable. Later, after the Munich crisis, the same official position—in other words, his identification with the government and in particular with T. G. Masaryk—was the cause of his sudden retreat from glory. Shortly before, Čapek had attacked fascism in his *Bílá nemoc* [The white plague, 1937]; this attack was well understood by all concerned. It was known that the name of the fascist industrialist, a character patterned on the German industrialist Krupp, had to be changed before the first performance of the play at the intervention of the German Embassy in Prague.

Čapek's play *Matka* [The mother, 1938], an appeal for the defense of Czechoslovakia, written and produced a few months before his death, underlined his decision to offer his services to his country. This literary *Guernica*, lesser known than the paint-

3. "*Nezaměstnanost*" [Unemployment], "*Systém*" [The system], "*Pšenice*" [The wheat].

4. Olga Scheinpflugová, *Český román* (Prague, 1947), p. 361.

ing, had similar urgency and timing. Čapek must have had Spain in mind when he gave to the central character of the play, the mother, the name of Dolores; her husband died in the military service in Africa, a fact which would be most improbable if he were a Czech. The play was successfully produced in Russia in 1939, a year after its Prague premiere. *Pravda* of 30 June 1939 brought out a review in which Karel Čapek was called "goriaschii patriot"—a fervent patriot. Other reviews of *Matka*, like that in *Kniga i revoliutsia*,[5] mentioned Gorki's *Mat'* (*Mother*) and Brecht's *Gewehre der Frau Carrar*.

During the political crisis preceding Munich, Čapek tried desperately to arouse an interest in the situation of Czechoslovakia. He addressed himself to his confreres, but soon learned that very few literary friendships formed in prosperity could survive the trial of ill fortune. The international world of intellectuals, whom Čapek used to meet at congresses in Geneva or Budapest, appeared deaf to his plea for at least verbal support of the threatened Czechoslovak democracy. If Čapek's works received no response from his colleagues in the West, they certainly were heard by the Germans. With the signature of Munich, the fate of the author of *Bílá nemoc* and the friend of T. G. Masaryk was doomed. Čapek died of influenza at Christmas, 1938. Had it not been so, he most probably would have died in a concentration camp, as did his brother and coauthor, and some of his close friends.

In the antifascist world, the political impact of Čapek's *Bílá nemoc* and *Matka* stirred an interest in his other works. During the late thirties a new Russian translation of *Válka s mloky* [War with the newts] appeared, the work which was and remains a favorite with the Russians. "On [Čapek] interesen i blizok sovietskomu chitatelu" (He is interesting for the Soviet reader).[6]

5. M. Semenov, "*Poslednoe slovo Karela Chapeka* (Mat')," *Kniga i revoliutsia*, vols. 5–6 (1939), pp. 156–58.

6. R. Zebina, "Izbrannyi Karel Chapek," *Zvezda*, 1948, no. 8.

Why? Because he knew how to expose the capitalist society, its policies, its misuse of technology—the robot is an evil power only as long as it is guided by the capitalist society[7]—its selfishness, cruelty, and stupidity. One of the reviewers[8] of the book reminds the reader that the time of *Válka s mloky* is the time of the international appeasement policy and underlines Čapek's skill in portraying "salamandry fashisty," the destructive forces of the capitalist technology. However, continues the article, the satirist disregarded the element of revolution as a solution to the problems he was treating. Čapek is compared with H. G. Wells and one reviewer even mentioned Swift.[9] In those short articles commenting on Čapek's early translations into Russian, he is already presented in a standard Marxist form: as the critic of the capitalist world and as the enemy of fascism. With these words of commendation, due reservation must be made for his failure to reach a positive solution and to join the forces of the proletarian revolution. It was to be on the strength of these points that Čapek's work would be accepted both in Soviet Russia and in Communist Czechoslovakia.

While *Válka s mloky* was published in Russia, in Czechoslovakia in 1939 the silence surrounding its author was complete. His books were banned not because they were "entartet" (degenerate), but because they represented the period which the German occupation wished to eradicate (*ausrotten, ausradieren*) from the Czech memory. Of course Čapek's work continued to be read by his devotees. Nevertheless, even some of those turned their interest to a literature which might propose other than pragmatic answers to the questions which were in their minds. The world around was one of nightmare and fear, and Čapek's

7. I. A. Bernshtein, "Karel Chapek v Sovetskom Soiuze," in *Chekhoslovatsko sovetskie literaturnye sviazi* (Moscow, 1964) p. 39.

8. B. Etingin, "Voina s salamandrami," *Literaturnoe obozrenie*, 1938, no. 13–14, pp. 76–80.

9. R. Aleksandrov in *Literaturnyi sovremennik*, 1938, no. 9.

utopia and his bonhomie lost their luster, at least for the time. In the aftermath of World War II, in the tense atmosphere of liberation, Čapek's previous authority seemed distant. True, the successor of Masaryk, Eduard Beneš, returned as president of the East-liberated Czechoslovakia. Yet, had it not been for a small volume of poetry written by his brother Josef in the concentration camp from which he never returned, Karel Čapek's name would hardly have been mentioned. After a short period of intellectual freedom, which included not merely Josef Čapek's poetry, but for example a translation of one of T. S. Eliot's poems or an essay in existentialism, the control of literary production set in. The Czechoslovak literati were involved in situations which directly affected their personal and literary existence; the foremost poets of the nation, Nezval and Seifert, wrote incidental verse on the liberation of Czechoslovakia by the Russian forces. In the tumult of those weeks and months, no one had leisure to occupy his mind with Karel Čapek and to think of reinstating him to his former rank. And when the dust settled in 1948, it became clear that he did not measure up to the literary requirements of the Stalinist period; his identification with the 1918–38 Czechoslovak Republic made him persona non grata once more. Czechoslovak literature stood on the threshold of a new, Eastern-oriented cultural era.

Čapek's past was not as anti-Soviet as one might suppose. In 1936 he praised the draft of the new Soviet Constitution. His comment was published in *Pravda* on 18 June 1936 under the headline "Zarubezhnye otliki na publikovanie proekta novoi konstitutsii SSSR" [International reactions on the publication of the draft of the new Soviet Constitution]. The interview was given over the telephone, and Čapek called the Soviet Constitution a milestone in European history, a bulwark against fascism, a "new type of democracy." In the past, Čapek had been known for his reluctance to sign leftist proclamations. In 1936, however, in his growing anxiety about the future of Czechoslovakia, he was ready to lend his name to political propaganda. He was looking for an ally in the political danger closing around his country. In the same year another interview with him was published in the popular Russian magazine *Ogonek*.[10] It appeared in the series "Chto dlia vas SSSR?" [What does the USSR mean to you?] together with opinions of such Czech writers as Communists Josef Kopta and František Kubka. In 1936–38, the Russians approached Čapek as a valuable international asset in their struggle against fascism. *Internatsional'naia literatura* (1937, no. 11) published an article about Čapek written by the old-guard Czech Communist, Bedřich Václavek. Two years later the same periodical had another writeup about him signed by Louis Aragon. In 1938, at the International Congress of Writers in Madrid, Alexei Tolstoy spoke of Čapek as of an intellectual who opposed fascist aggression.

All this fell into oblivion during the Stalinist literary deepfreeze. With its thaw, however, the ban on Karel Čapek was lifted. His name survived the cataclysms of the political-literary life behind the Iron Curtain and rose to a new prominence. During the late fifties and early sixties there appeared a series of informative Russian bibliographies of Czechoslovak authors, including Karel Čapek. He was raised to the rank of "nashi druz'ia" (our friends) to speak in terms of the contemporary Slavic *Wechselseitigkeit*. Čapek's Russian bibliography[11] gives a complete list of Russian translations and works about him. The first translation, *RUR*, has the date 1924, followed by *Anglické listy* in 1925. Most impressive is a recent five-volume edition of his collected works (1958–59). The text of the bibliography once more focuses on Čapek's satire on the capitalist world. The writer is well acquainted with the political atmosphere of Čapek's time: "Pust'salamandry, lish' by ne marksisty" (Let them be newts but not Marxists).[12] Many extreme right-wingers, in Czechoslovakia

10. *Ogonek*, 1936, no. 8–9.

11. *Karel Chapek*, Bio-bibliograficheskii ukazatel' (Moscow, 1959).

12. Ibid., p. 14.

and in other parts of Europe, felt precisely that way when Čapek was writing and publishing his utopia about the newts.

At the time of these manifestations of Čapek's literary rehabilitation, a major collective work on the history of Czechoslovak literature was under way. Its publication (1963) gave Čapek a space reserved for the foremost authors. The essay on Čapek in *Ocherki istorii cheshskoi literatury XIX–XX vekov*[13] was written by S. V. Nikol'skii, the Russian specialist on him. His monograph *Karel Chapek* was translated into Czech in 1952. No Communist critic, whether he is Russian or Czech, will dissent from this official model criticism, not even the most independent of all, the Slovak Alexander Matuška. Simplified and condensed, Nikol'skii's essay rests on three cardinal points: 1) Čapek's criticism of the capitalist society, 2) his opposition to fascism, 3) his incapacity to break away from the mentality of bourgeois democracy. Nikol'skii divided Čapek's work into four periods: 1920–25, the groping of his early writings; 1925–34, the years of Čapek's "officialdom" and his relationship with T. G. Masaryk; and finally the critical years 1934–38, eloquent of Čapek's antifascist stand. The original author of this division is the Czech Communist critic Bedřich Václavek[14] who was the first to emphasize Čapek's attack on capitalist society and his inability to accept the Marxist revolution as the solution of the world crisis. The essay on Karel Čapek in *Ocherki* is seventeen pages long. In comparison with Czech studies, it is rigidly Marxist and somehow colorless, but since it appears in a standard literary history this was to be expected. More alive is the study by I. A. Bernshtein, "Karel Chapek v Sovetskom Soiuze" [Karel Čapek in Soviet Russia].[15]

13. [Essays on Czech literature of the nineteenth and twentieth centuries] (Moscow, 1963); henceforth *Ocherki*.

14. Bedřich Václavek, *Česká literatura XX. století* (Prague, 1947), pp. 95, 96. Part of this work was orginally published as an article in 1935.

15. In *Chekhoslovatsko sovetskie literaturnye sviazi* (Moscow, 1964).

The influence of World War I on Čapek seems to be exaggerated by Russian and Czech critics equally. Of course Karel Čapek and his brother Josef—his close collaborator at that time—were affected by the war. Josef feared that in spite of his bad sight he might be drafted; many of the brothers' literary friends went to the front and some did not return. Nevertheless, reading the brothers' war correspondence with S. K. Neumann,[16] one might be surprised at how little Karel Čapek seems to have been involved in the political events of those years. This does not mean that he was not aware of their importance. Still, his artist's interest obviously prevailed over the pressures of war. During those years Čapek worked on his doctorate in philosophy, and it was through those studies that he acquired an outlook on life along the lines of American pragmatism and behaviorism.

Nikol'skii, and other Russians and Czechs as well, see the dominant theme of Čapek's work as the confrontation of modern technology with mankind. In the opinion of Nikol'skii, Čapek was unable to solve this problem with finality because he was treating it "vnesotsial'o"—outside its social (class) context. This proposition and all that it involves were accepted by the Russians and Czechs as the major perspective in which Čapek's work has to be approached. His reluctance to accept revolution is seen as the obstacle to reaching the right conclusions. "Chapek ne vidit klassovo . . ." (Čapek is unable to see [society] in terms of social class).[17]

His relationship with T. G. Masaryk—evo blizost' k burzhuaznoi masarikovskoi ideologii[18]—is treated as another regrettable development. Although the "realisticheskaia konkretnost'" of the period 1925–34 is highly praised, it is labeled as "superficial." The Soviet critic A. Gurovich[19] has not a word of praise for the

16. *Viktor Dyk, S. K. Neumann, bratří Čapkové.*

17. Mints and Malevich, *K. Chapek i A. N. Tolstoi*, p. 130.

18. Bernshtein, "Karel Chapek v Sovetskom Soiuze," p. 37.

19. A. Gurovich, in *Chekhoslovatsko sovetskie literaturnye sviazi*, p. 65.

two books of short stories, *Povídky z jedné kapsy* and *Povídky z druhé kapsy* (1929), which in their own genre are the most accomplished fiction that ever came out of Čapek's workshop. Recently they were translated into English (*Tales from Two Pockets*)[20] and they seem to have stood the trial of time very well, indeed better than his other, more ambitious work. True, some of the journalistic facility which Čapek achieved at that time makes one wonder if by any chance at least a part of the above Russian statement could not be true. The Czech Marxists may eventually accept the "superficial" quality of some aspects of Čapek's work. On the other hand, they will instinctively, and as well as they can, keep aloof from the Russian (Nikol'skii's) effort to present Čapek as a collaborator in Masaryk's "demagogic" concept of a Czechoslovak Republic. Nikol'skii went so far as to claim that Čapek in writing *Hovory s T. G. Masarykem* took the part of press-secretary between the president and the nation. Nikol'skii added that Masaryk misguided Čapek by his "lzhesotsialism" (false socialism and false humanism); further, that it was Masaryk who warned Čapek before the Revolution.

Here, once more, the Czech and Slovak critics seem reluctant to follow their Russian colleague. The voluminous Czech monograph[21] on Čapek's intellectual profile avoids the issue; it hardly mentions *Hovory s T. G. Masarykem*. Branžovský characterized Masaryk's and Čapek's weltanschauung as an "abstract bourgeois humanism."[22] He modified his vague statement by adding that the prewar Masaryk and his realism appeared to the young Čapek "academically" remote. For many Czechs, whether they are intellectuals or not, the history of the First Czechoslovak Republic with its Masaryk and Čapek, its Czech Legions in Russia, France, and Italy during World War I, remains emo-

20. Paul Selver, trans. (London: The Folio Society, 1962).

21. Josef Branžovský, *Karel Čapek, světový názor a umění* (Prague, 1963).

22. Ibid., p. 129.

tionally close. For the Russians, of course, no such inhibition exists; on the contrary, they have every reason to support the Communist myth that Czechoslovakia has enjoyed democratic freedom only since 1945–48. Nikol'skii's formulations, such as "the collapse of the Czechoslovak democracy" or his sentence about the Czech parliamentary fascism, might leave a bad taste even for a Czech Communist.

The last period of Čapek's life and work receive a unanimous and sincere accolade both from the Russians and the Czechs. Čapek's disillusionment with the West, particularly with England, the country which before had held his sympathies and admiration, did not pass unnoticed. Čapek's shock in finding Czechoslovakia isolated from its previous allies—a shock which the whole nation felt—pushed him toward a revision of his political views. It was then that he wrote his comment on the draft for the new Soviet Constitution published in *Pravda*. None of the Marxist critics will ever omit mention of this event.

The Czech variants on the Russian criticism of Čapek are many; they appear as introductions or afterwords to the new editions of his works in the form of articles or books. We will consider three representative monographs, two of them written by Czechs, the third by a Slovak. The most conformist of the three has the unimaginative title *Karel Čapek*[23] and was written by I. Klíma, who approximates Nikol'skii, though without the latter's poise and authority. Klíma formulates anew what had already been said or what one expects to be said, on the subject. He contends that Čapek refuted the idea of the class society and this in spite of the fact that this society existed around him.[24] For Klíma, perhaps the most negative aspect of Čapek's work is his effort to separate great ideals from everyday life. Čapek's advice to work well and not to trouble oneself with great ideas

23. Ivan Klíma, *Karel Čapek* (Prague, 1962).

24. Ibid., p. 5.

(thus you will contribute to the welfare of mankind) was rejected by Klíma as the attitude of "the hero in decline."

There can be no doubt that, with the exception of the last period of his life, Čapek loathed the concept of the heroic call. In 1913 he wrote that literature is saturated with descriptions of "beautiful passions" and that formulation of social problems like that of Gheon's *Le Pain* should attract an artist's attention.[25] Not made for heroic action, Čapek's protagonists oppose any violent extremes. Only his last play, *Matka*, calls for sacrifice and courage in the fight against fascism and aggression, and only then does Čapek meet with unadulterated Marxist approval. His sudden conversion in the face of the immediate danger threatening his country received full praise. It is because of this attitude that he was called "borets antifashist" (fighter against fascism) by I. A. Bernshtein.[26] The Slovak critic Alexander Matuška considers this volte-face a worthy decision: Čapek chose the dangerous commitment not merely for his heroes but also for himself.[27] For the Communist mind the idea of the play does not lose its attractiveness even in our days. In 1964 it was performed in Frunze, Kirgizia.

Čapek's pessimism—a variety of pragmatic relativism—was criticized already during his lifetime. For the Russians, this pessimism and relativism is the weak point of his work. It is not difficult to discover that Čapek's optimistic reassurances have their counterpart. While he was writing for the newspaper, while he was proposing a "philosophy" of life, Čapek displayed a "healthy" optimism; left without the light of ratiocination, his artist's views became clouded. What can be more hopeless and dreary than some situations and persons of his early short stories, such as those collected in *Boží muka* [Wayside cross] and *Trapné povídky* [Tales of distress]? In their entirety they express the

25. Přehled, 1913, no. 12, pp. 53–54.

26. Bernshtein, "Karel Chapek v Sovetskom Soiuze," p. 53.

27. Alexander Matuška, *Pokus o Karla Čapka* (Bratislava, 1963), p. 336.

impossibility of escaping one's existence of quiet desperation. Man stands fascinated and unable to resolve the mystery of a footstep in the snow or of a sentence scribbled on the wall above his head. He helplessly faces adultery, theft, harsh words—in fine, the reality of life. That this part of Čapek's work, from which he separated himself in his later years, found little response in Marxist criticism is self-evident. The Marxist critic, however, must find and does find a positive explanation: all that happened in *Boží muka* or *Trapné povídky* happened in the capitalist world, where a pessimistic outlook inevitably penetrates and colors the work of the bourgeois artist.

Josef Branžovský's monograph is focused on the intellectual side of Čapek's work. Branžovský discusses Čapek's dependence on American pragmatism and behaviorism. They suited him, Branžovský explains, as a philosophy which did not enforce separation "between the street and the classroom";[28] in other words, they permitted Čapek to use both experience and speculation. Pragmatism was responsible for Čapek's rejection of "absolutes," not because they are necessarily "untrue," but because they might prove worthless as "working tools." Like James and Dewey, Čapek hoped that the democratic society might be saved with reforms.[29] Branžovský further criticizes Čapek for his failure to seize the connection between "the negative symptoms of civilization and capitalism."[30]

Klíma also objected to Čapek's identification of technology with the power behind it. And he found a good argument in saying that without modern technology it is impossible to fight poverty, famine, and disease. It is the power behind the technological know-how which has to be scrutinized. Like bourgeois artists, Čapek was incapable of making a valid diagnosis of the ailments of the world around him and instead of blaming capital-

28. Branžovský, *Karel Čapek, světový názor a umění*, p. 35.

29. Ibid., p. 47; Klíma described it as an effort "to save the petty bourgeois."

30. Ibid., p. 105; see also p. 128.

ism was accusing civilization. Yet he envisioned the dangers of an "imperialist" technological warfare. Branžovský reminds us—and this is a very pertinent reminder—that Čapek started to write *Válka s mloky* under the impact of the negotiation between Mussolini, Laval, and Eden. But Čapek omitted telling his reader the very reasons which pushed the Western powers to compromise with fascism: the intent to strengthen the future aggressor against the Soviet Union.[31] In Branžovský's interpretation, *Bílá nemoc* is an attack on the greediness and ruthless struggle for power of the capitalist society (as is *Ze života hmyzu* [The insect play]). In *Bílá nemoc* thc petty bourgeois, though frightened by the white plague, is nevertheless pleased when two of his competitors are removed by the disease. The young people who are immune to the plague do not care about the dying; at least there will be more opportunities for themselves. The upper-class bourgeois, the industrialist baron Krüg, identifies his business interests with the interest of the country and does not hide the fact that he has means to buy the press to write either for peace or for war. The conflict between Dr. Galen, the physician who refuses to place his remedy for the white plague at the disposal of medical science unless he is given guarantees that the war will not start, and the warmonger Krüg, is a conflict between humanism and power on the surface only. Čapek's humanism (Dr. Galen's) and the man of power (Krüg) are shaped out of bourgeois concepts. The hero of *Bílá nemoc*, Dr. Galen, failed in his struggle against the white plague because he attacked it as an isolated individual and not as a member of the socialist collective;[32] his humanism was ineffective because it was democratic humanism, which has to be distinguished from the efficacious proletarian humanism. Čapek approached the problem as a conflict of ideas and not as an issue of the class struggle.[33] He

31. Ibid., p. 226; see also B. Etingin, "Voina s salamandrami."

32. Branžovský, *Karel Čapek*, p. 239.

33. Ibid., p. 241.

separated what Branžovský would not: the capitalist structure of the bourgeois democracy and its humanism. It was this bourgeois limitation which prevented Čapek from reaching greatness, continues Branžovský; his social class was no longer capable of a monumental synthesis.[34] The Russians Mints and Malevich expressed this thought as "the lack of the monolithic structure characteristic of the twentieth-century society."[35]

Another example of Branžovský's Marxist interpretation was chosen from *Povídky z jedné kapsy*. The story "Zločin v chalupě" [The crime in a cottage] is about a peasant who murdered his father-in-law because he sold a piece of land, the loss of which endangered the prosperity of the farm. The peasant, seconded by the whole community, describes his father-in-law as a stubborn fool and does not deny the murder; but he refuses to plead guilty. He did merely what was every man's duty: he defended the prosperity of the farm. Čapek aimed at a case for the ambivalence of the human concept of what is just (the main theme of his novel *Hordubal*). Branžovský added: the bourgeois mentality is unable to disclose the true reason of the evil; the criminal of the bourgeois society will disappear only with the dissolution of the bourgeois society.[36] We have to agree with Branžovský insofar as the particular crime described in Čapek's short story is concerned: it would not, because it could not, take place in the society of collective farming. The father-in-law could not sell the field since it would belong to the collective. The Marxist critic views the society in which Čapek's short story took place as a closed historical period and considers it futile to be its reformer. Branžovský explains that it would be a "primitive" approach to identify Čapek with Živnostenská banka or Dr. Preiss[37]—for a Czech Communist both are eloquent symbols of

34. Ibid., p. 261.

35. Mints and Malevich, *Chapek i A. N. Tolstoi*, p. 133.

36. Branžovský, *Karel Čapek*, p. 165.

37. Ibid., p. 268.

Czech capitalism—and cites Lenin, whose interpretation of L. N. Tolstoy might be used for Čapek too: in spite of contradictions inherent in a literary work created in the bourgeois society, its artistic qualities might survive it. This does not mean that a literary work should be isolated from its class origins, it merely states that in spite of his class limitations a writer could be a "decent person" and a good artist, especially when his class denomination has become a part of history.[38] On the grounds of this theory the Russians and the Czechs might read and enjoy their classics and proudly point back to their past literature.

Among the existing criticism on Čapek, *Pokus o Karla Čapka* [An essay on Karel Čapek, 1963] by Alexander Matuška stands out vividly. The work is not a compilation nor does it anxiously follow the Marxist blueprint. The ever-present monitor did not paralyze Matuška's judgment and sensibility, as it so often did his colleagues'. In general, he seems to be less inclined to use the citations of a representative of Czech Communism like Gottwald, Nejedlý, or Fučík—in short, the authorities of the Stalinist period. He seems to undertake his task quite uninhibitedly. He reexamines what he and his generation were taught in the schools, first of Czechoslovakia, then Tiso's Slovakia, and finally Stalinist Czechoslovakia. He is a Marxist to be sure; nevertheless, he and his peers started a quest for literary values which they might call their own. It is revealing to compare Matuška's essay on Čapek with some other contemporary criticism on Čapek, for example, Jan Kopecký's afterword to a new edition of Čapek's plays; one is immediately aware of the difference between a writer who is conscious of party line and a younger man who is much less anxious to conform. It is not without significance that Matuška is a Slovak and that his voice is heard at the time of the Slovak protest against "the cult of the personality." The new refreshing tone of Matuška's monograph derives not merely

38. Ibid., p. 270; see also Karel Čapek, *Poznámky o tvorbě*, afterword by Jiří Brabec (Prague, 1959).

from his apparent ease in dealing with his subject within the framework of the Marxist literary theory, but also from his talent for making its limitations as flexible as he wished. When he writes about Čapek's relationship to other movements in European literature, such as expressionism, futurism, cubism, and unanimism, Matuška is not satisfied with loosely applied adjectives like "cubist" but gives a fair account of how cubism applies to Čapek's work.[39] He cites names of German expressionists like E. Blass, G. Heym, and P. Zeehl, whom one might not find in the indexes of other essays on Čapek. His comparative stock-in-trade is also distinguished. He would parallel a scene from *Ze života hmyzu* with a passage from Voltaire's *Micromegas*. Matuška points out that Čapek's Tulák (the vagabond), indignant over the bellicose insects, has a line which echoes what Voltaire's Sirian had said in a similar situation: "Il me prend d'envie . . . d'écraser de trois coups de pied toute cette fourmilière d'assassins ridicules."[40] By his comparison, Matuška brings into relief the intellectual character of Čapek's work, which tends to subordinate the imaginative and emotional element to the rational. The Čapek-Voltaire parallel reveals something about the former: like Voltaire, he relied on his intellect, and his work was often a mere comment on ideas expressed with stylistic grace. "The fighting Voltaire eventually takes refuge in his garden, the peaceful Čapek might leave his garden and fight."[41]

Matuška gives the political-literary account of the milieu which faced the young Čapek. The year 1920 saw Mussolini's march on Rome; in 1921, *RUR* was published; in 1923, Hitler's *putsch* took place in Munich. In 1924, Lenin died and it was the

39. Matuška, *Pokus o Karla Čapka* (Bratislava, 1963), pp. 17, 18, 268, 305.

40. Ibid., p. 25. *Micromegas* was translated into Czech in 1851; the translator was K. Havlíček, an intellectual who is no less important for the development of modern Czech thought than Karel Čapek. Karel Havlíček Borovský, *Některé pověsti* (Kutná Hora, 1851).

41. Matuška, *Pokus o Karla Čapka*, p. 27.

year of the Locarno conference; also in 1924, Joyce's *Ulysses* and Gide's *Les Faux-Monnayeurs* appeared and in 1929, *Im Westen nichts Neues* by Remarque. The Czech list is even more eloquent of Čapek's world, although it might say little to any but the Czech reader.[42] "Čapek will never sing the world of modern technology as Marinetti does," remarked Matuška, "because he is rather afraid of it."[43] His technological world was an ambiguous one: he was attracted by its "machinery" and "concreteness" as were painters or poets contemporary with him—such as Marinetti or the Czech S. K. Neumann. On the other hand, he was "frightened" by the dehumanization which technology might impose on human life. In every one of Čapek's utopias, nature and civilization are conflicting.[44] Yet—and here Matuška agrees with other Marxist critics—Čapek would always advocate reform and never revolution.[45] This does not come as a surprise, since "revolution" is an extreme which Čapek attacks from every position: "the word 'overthrow' or 'revolution' reminds us mostly of something which is destructive, overpowering and against nature, something which is outside the natural and reasonable order of things."[46] Matuška used the word "fearful" (*bojazlivo*) for Čapek's attitude, and another Czech critic of the prewar generation, Václav Černý, wrote in 1936 about Čapek in similar terms: "the life which he [Čapek] praises is in reality the life of a frightened [*bojácný*] man."[47] Čapek belonged to the capitalist society, he criticized it, and he was never able to dissociate himself from it. The menace of modern technology as he conceived it threatened both bourgeois and proletarian. Technology might sharpen the social conflicts, concedes Matuška, but it has no say in their solution.[48]

42. Ibid., p. 54.

43. Ibid., p. 168.

44. Ibid., p. 197.

45. Ibid., p. 195.

46. Čapek, *Sloupkový gambit* (Prague, 1957), p. 95.

47. Václav Černý, *Karel Čapek* (Prague, 1936), p. 19.

48. Matuška, *Pokus o Karla Čapka*, pp. 201–9.

Matuška also noticed that Čapek's modern science and its technology have two faces. In his newspaper articles—such as the paragraphs dedicated to Mme Curie and reprinted in *Ratolest a vavřín* [Twig and laurel]—Čapek writes lyrical praise of atomic research; in his fiction on the contrary, as in *Továrna na absolutno* [The Absolute at large], he wishes to exorcise the world which the same science is helping to build. Writing about the exhibition of the British Empire (in *Anglické listy*) Čapek is impressed by the modern technology: "The machines are sumptuous . . . , but the life of those used for their production and upkeep is far from sumptuous."[49] Nearly everyone of Čapek's interpreters brought forth this passage, including the Russians Nikol'skii and Bernshtein, and the Czech Fučík. Matuška commented that both Čapek and Engels saw the condition of the English working class, both wrote about it with eloquence; the sole difference was that Engels understood what he saw and drew adequate conclusions from it, whereas Čapek turned away from the logic of his own premises.[50] Moreover, he explained openly why he was not a Communist and continued to assert that poverty imposes moral and not social obligations.[51] He would use a sentence like "the world does not need hatred" in defense of his unwillingness to join the class struggle.[52]

One must expect such reservations from a man committed to pragmatism and its tolerance. Čapek's dislike of any uncompromising position (his attacks on clericalism or nationalism) derives not merely from his intellectual orientation—as Matuška thinks—but even more from his temperament. The tone of intellectual inquiry was natural to him. His rare attempts to express emotion were never very successful; then he might lapse into conventional images for which he blamed other writers.

49. Čapek, *Anglické listy* (London, 1951), p. 49.

50. Matuška, *Pokus o Karla Čapka*, p. 213.

51. Čapek, *Proč nejsem komunistou* (Munich, 1957), pp. 8, 16.

52. Matuška, *Pokus o Karla Čapka*, p. 215.

Abandoning his Voltairian style, Čapek would speak about stars for grandeur and about thyme for homeland. Matuška does not leave this unnoticed. He underlines the rationalist character of his author and his difficulty in expressing not merely the lyricism of emotions but particularly that of nature. This contradicts Čapek's interest and occupation with nature as we know it from his *Zahradníkův rok* [The gardener's year]. In a way, Čapek enjoyed being a journalist more than being a writer. At times he seemed to prefer journalism to his fiction, and his fiction was often the work of a publicist rather than that of a "poet." Journalism supported his contact with people, it suited his belief in the importance of the everyday life, and enforced the active, pragmatist, optimist attitude. Matuška demonstrated convincingly how journalism influenced Čapek's fiction and vice versa and how they often contradicted each other.[53]

When Čapek was traveling in Spain, like every tourist he went to see a corrida—*Výlet do Španěl* [The journey to Spain]. The spectacle filled him both with disgust and admiration. Matuška cites his "letter" from Spain as an example of Čapek's double experience. There is more to it. It is not merely an ambivalent intellectual operation; it is also a constitutional ambivalence, which some may call Freudian. Čapek likes to identify himself with the little man and his mediocrity, in short with all that is the opposite of passion, violence, and heroism. He advocates ideas relevant to this happy mediocrity. And all of a sudden he sees his little man (at the corrida) as a spectator in the spectacular theater of life and death—and passionately enjoying it. Čapek finds this theater and its highly pitched pathos simply revolting. And at the same time something in him, perhaps the artist, is touched by the "heroic" quality inherent in a good corrida. It touches something which, either by necessity or by choice, he never allowed to enter his life.

Great gestures, whether they were words or action, had little

53. Ibid., pp. 64, 71.

place in Čapek's world. For this reason he would remain cold to the poetry of a Racine or Corneille. He poked fun at the hero of history (*Napoleon*, 1933) as well as at the tragedy of sentiment (*Romeo a Julie*, 1932). Like Voltaire—to borrow Matuška's reference—he would use wit to make pathos digestible. Matuška found sources for it in the Jamesian pragmatism, but this is true in part only, for Čapek's temperament was also responsible. Moreover, what else than his temperament makes man adopt certain intellectual attitudes? Just as telling as Čapek's corrida experience were his literary dislikes; Matuška named them with understanding. For instance, Čapek considered Joyce "znepokojivý a vulgární" (vulgar and disturbing), which is but another qualification of what he said about the corrida.

Better than any other bourgeois or Marxist critic, Matuška observed Čapek's difficulty in his relationship with his fellow man. Čapek glorifies him, whether he be a miner—as in *První parta* [The first rescue party]—or a handyman who comes to his house, whether he meets him on his way to the newspaper office or sits with him in a trolley car. Yet he never dares to come near enough to touch him. And it is precisely at this point that Čapek as an artist is vulnerable. Matuška's formulation is slightly different, but he too sensed well the ambiguity of Čapek's relationship with his neighbor: a mixture of love and disgust, of condescension and fear.[54] This applies also to Čapek's dealing with the collective. In *RUR* it is the anonymous collective of robots which threatens the representatives of the human race. A part of Čapek's refusal of revolutionary solutions must have had its motivation in his dread and fear of the human mass.[55] In his memorable confession, *Why I Am Not a Communist*, he said that he did not believe in the value of masses; they are mere tools for achievement of power and material for political ends.[56] Čapek's

54. Ibid., p. 299.

55. Ibid., p. 210.

56. Čapek, *Proč nejsem komunistou*, p. 9.

characters, according to Matuška, are vehicles for the idea of a play or novel.[57] Čapek preferred the type to the individual; his description of a person and his habitat are often reduced to a mere detail (often linguistic) leaving no place for nuances. Without trying to be ironical, Matuška wrote that Čapek's portrayal of Dashenka (Čapek's dog) is more complicated than his portraiture of man.[58]

As the relation between reality and works of art plays a major role in Marxist literary esthetics, Čapek's critics, Branžovský and Nikol'skii, refer to the hackneyed cliché of bourgeois society imposing an estrangement between the artist and the reality surrounding him. Matuška's formulation pierced through the flat statement of the Marxist tenet: the modern "abstract" art and its difficulty of being "understood" is a subjective answer of the artist to the complexity and contradiction of the capitalist society in which he lives. The artist answers the present complex situation by writing poetry and painting pictures which are as complicated and multiple (and therefore "obscure") as the reality which confronts him. This interpretation of modern art applies of course to the early period of Čapek's and not to his later work. Here perhaps is the place to quote an opinion of a dissenter from the current criticism on Čapek: "Strangely enough, the works that made Čapek's name famous all over the world do not reach the level of those which preceded them."[59] By these the critic Václav Černý means Čapek's early play *Loupežník* [The robber] and fiction such as *Trapné povídky* [Tales of distress], *Boží muka* [Wayside cross] and *Zářivé hlubiny* [The glowing depths], all of them reflecting the complexity of human existence—or "pessimistic relativism" as a Russian critic might put it. At the conclusion of his monograph, Matuška raises the question of whether or not Čapek was a great writer. He answers:

57. Matuška, *Pokus o Karla Čapka*, p. 304.

58. Ibid., p. 303.

59. Černý, *Karel Čapek*, p. 13.

Čapek's work stands for the values of "obyčejný život" (everyday life, common life); thus his negation of any "greatness," whether literary or live, has set limitations on his own work. Marxist critics treated Čapek harshly, Matuška adds, because they wished him to be elsewhere than he was, in the bourgeois world. This is an unchangeable fact; yet his work, including its typically bourgeois aspects (evident in *Zahradníkův rok*, for example), continues to be a milestone in the history of Czech literature.[60]

"We read quite often: 'What a pity that an author of Čapek's talent was not equipped with the "scientific" weltanschauung!' It might be so . . . , yet what a pity that the authors who possess this advantage did not write anything which could match either *První parta* or *Válka s mloky*."[61] This quotation, fringing on ideological heresy, was written by the successful Czech playwright Pavel Kohout; it is from the introduction to *Válka s mloky*, which Kohout adapted for the theater and which was played with great success in Prague. Kohout rewrote Čapek's utopia in the light of the contemporary threat of nuclear war. Čapek's attack on capitalist society often softened, especially in places where it touched the "little man" and his life. After twenty-five years, Kohout's adaptation is sharper and grimmer. The dialogue quoted below gives a good indication of Kohout's high opinion of Čapek and his belief in the permanency of Čapek's work.

| | |
|---|---|
| *Bondy* (*an actor*): | Where is the author! |
| *Chief reporter:* | Don't you know, Sir, that he died long ago? Out of sheer sorrow. But he told you what will happen. |
| *Bright* (*an actor*): | If he died how can this play go on? |
| *Chief reporter:* | This is a particular feature of literary works whose authors were right. |

60. Matuška, *Pokus o Karla Čapka*, pp. 321, 341, 342.

61. Čapek, *Válka s mloky*, adapted by Pavel Kohout (Prague, 1963), p. 14.

The Czech and Russian reevaluation of Čapek pronounced him "the classic of modern Czech literature." The Russian pronouncement sounds an impersonal note, whereas the Czechs—the playwright Kohout or the critic Matuška—seem to be personally involved in the rehabilitation of their author. Yet from whatever standpoint they and the others wrote, they all closed their investigation with the unanimous decree that Čapek is a great asset to modern Czech literature.

# 5
# THE CZECH SOCIALIST REALISTS

*There can be no worse theoretician of art than the State.*

Alberto Moravia

IF YOU happen to open a Czech or Russian history of Czech literature dealing with the years 1918–45, you would inevitably come across three writers who stand above the crowd: S. K. Neumann (1875–1947), I. Olbracht (1875–1959), and Marie Majerová (1883–1962). Others might rise, but these three would never cede their leading position. From a certain point of view one might consider the work of Marie Majerová as the most telling of the three, since her fiction and the ideology behind it testify to her unremitting devotion to the socialist idea and to the party. She is the least original writer of the group, yet the most dedicated. It is not without importance that she was born and grew up in the proletarian class and that part of her education was acquired in evening courses for workers. She is the self-made intellectual, "the type of artist deeply rooted in the working class . . . not one who joined it from the outside."[1] Her biography reflects the history of the socialist movement, first in Austria and later in Czechoslovakia. The potential conflict between the intellectual-artist and the party man did not touch

1. Jiří Hájek, *Národní umělkyně Marie Majerová* (Prague, 1952), p. 11.

her mind. When in 1929 she signed a protest against the new look of the party, it was a mere error of judgment, perhaps the influence of a friend. All this was understood and rewarded accordingly. In 1945 Majerová became editor of the periodical *Československo*, which presented official teachings and propaganda. In 1947 she was awarded the honor of National Artist, a title which the Czech critic Hájek chose for his monograph about her. Her major novel, *Siréna* [Siren, 1935], was translated into German, French, and Russian; *Havířská balada* [Ballad of a miner, 1938] was recently published in English by the government export house Artia.

In her official status Majerová visited factories and mine districts and wrote enthusiastic reports about the achievements of the socialist Czechoslovakia. She would treat boldly subjects like the police dogs on the western border of the Iron Curtain and report on her visit to the Khrushchev family.[2] During her long career, she never wrote without the socialist idea in mind. Her early novel *Svět ze všech nejkrásnější* [The most beautiful world, 1923] is indeed conventional; in reading its first chapters and knowing that it is supposed to be the harbinger of Czech socialist realist fiction, one wonders how this could be true. The novel itself would have been long forgotten if it were not for its author's political position. Nevertheless, in spite of the novel's lurid sentimentality, its naive and dated feminism, the story, particularly in its 1951 edition, deals with the beginnings of the Czech socialist movement. When in the thirties the Marxist theory of socialist realism rose on the Czechoslovak literary horizon, it fitted Majerová like a glove. In contrast to other writers, she had to make little effort to conform to its tenets. While a Tilschová or Pujmanová was obliged to visit factories and mines to learn how to write about them, Majerová could merely remember. Olbracht, a much more competent writer than she, had to use his skill and imagination in creating a servant girl who

2. Marie Majerová, *Ševcovská polka a jiné radosti* (Prague, 1962), pp. 171–74.

became a militant Communist;[3] Majerová herself served as a maid in Budapest. Her stepfather worked in the coal district Kladno, and she was only in her teens when she took part in the miners' strike of 1900. Kladno became the locale for her novel *Sirêna.* Even without the communist propaganda this novel must be associated with socialist-oriented fiction. Although *Sirêna* may not be comparable to *Germinal*, it can well stand the comparison with *King Coal;* it is considered to be the classic of Czech socialist realism, "a work expressing our epoch."[4] No wonder that it was she and not any one else who was chosen to represent the Czech socialist realism. In her last collection of short stories, *Cesta blesku* [The path of lightning, 1954], everyone, young and old, glows with unselfish happiness and working zeal. The husband and wife never quarrel; their children start the blissful journey freehearted and later propose to themselves socialist goals surpassing even those of their model parents. The supervisors are fatherly and benevolent, and those who inadvertently make a mistake are always eager to reform. The volume, which contains fifteen short stories, instructs the reader in recent Czechoslovak history and enlarges upon the building-up period and the state's planned economy. All this is performed with great ease and on party-line premises.

Russian students of Czech literature frequently chose Majerová as the subject of their studies; R. R. Kuznetsova for instance, who translated *Sirêna* into Russian, wrote her dissertation on Majerová.[5] Yet, in spite of her popularity both at home and in Russia, Majerová's name usually follows those of S. K. Neumann and I. Olbracht.

S. K. Neumann's anarchist youth and his temperament, which was violently opposed to anything conservative, predestined him to be a Marxist. As a young man he attended workers' meetings

3. *Anna proletářka,* first published in Prague, 1928.

4. B. Václavek, *Tvorbou k realitě* (Prague, 1946), p. 115.

5. Garbinova published an essay and Smirnova and Patrushnikova wrote their seminar papers on her work.

and spent fourteen months in prison because of his activity with the group Omladina in 1893. Still, his past contained elements which had to be carefully screened by his Marxist critics before he could be described as the ideal image of the socialist realist poet. Such was, for example, the period of Neumann's association with the Czech decadent poets and their magazine *Moderní revue* (in 1897). The Czech and Russian critics treated this part of Neumann's literary biography carefully. Might it not be possible, for instance, to interpret the decadent "satanism" as a revolt against the existing social order? In her essay about Neumann, S. A. Sherlaimova wrote that he was never a true decadent; to support her opinion she cited F. X. Šalda, who saw Neumann as standing apart from his decadent generation, and who with astonishing foresight—it was in 1896—characterized Neumann's talent thus: his temperament responds quickly to ideas and his poetry is always ready to attack. It is evident that as a young man Neumann could not fail to be influenced by contemporary literary directions. He admired Whitman's free verse, his yes to modern civilization; he read Verhaeren and Baudelaire, *the* poet for the Czech decadents; and he was interested in cubism and futurism. In 1918, after he returned from World War I, Neumann was a member of the Czechoslovak Revolutionary Assembly (Národní shromáždění) and for a short time a government official. This, however, was the only political job of his career; as he himself confessed in his memoirs, he had neither talent nor desire to practice the art of politics, although his involvement in political life never diminished.[6] Soon he returned to literature and journalism; he was editor of the progressive literary magazines *Červen*, *Kmen*, and *Proletkult* and enrolled his poetry in the service of the Marxist revolution (*na sluzhbu revoliutsii*).[7]

In his collection of poetry *Rudé zpěvy* [Red songs, 1923], Neumann called himself "son of the revolution," and "brother of

6. S. K. Neumann, *Vzpomínky* (Prague, 1931), p. 83.
7. *Ocherki istorii cheshskoi literatury XIX–XX vekov*, p. 416.

the proletarian." In his poetic oratory of the time one may easily recognize the manner of Whitman or Maiakovskii. Like Maiakovskii he wrote *stikhi marshi,*—verse tuned to the march of revolution. The later editions of *Rudé zpěvy* contain the poem *Poděkování sovětskému svazu* [Thanksgiving to the Soviet Union], written in 1935 and echoing Maiakovskii's "millions" (*jsou už nás miliony*): "We are millions; we were slaves, now we are free, we, Czechs, Slovaks, Russians, Jews, Germans, Hungarians." *Zpěv zástupů* [Song of the crowds] adds to this socialist paean Indians, Turks, Negroes, and Chinese. Nothing is easier than to underestimate this type of poetry, especially since poets like Maiakovskii knew how to write on similar themes with originality. Yet sometimes poetry defies literary evaluation. During the Nazi occupation of Czechoslovakia, a woman waiting in prison for her death wrote to her family that she learned by heart Neumann's *Poděkování sovětskému svazu* and that these verses were her daily prayer, supported her hopes, and gave meaning to her life.[8] Such a confession is not a literary criterion, of course, although very few poets can boast that their words have been on the lips of one about to die.

Neumann, was a born dissenter and fighter. During the twenties he attacked Nezval and Teige because he felt that their poetry and the theory behind it betrayed the proletarian cause. In 1929 he himself was in opposition to the Czechoslovak Communist party, which he helped organize. For nearly a decade he was outside its ranks and when asked why he did not return sooner, said that what was good enough for Gorki and Maiakovskii was good enough for him.[9] The Russian critics never doubted Neumann's loyalty toward revolutionary ideas, his admiration for Soviet Russia, and his belief that it would bring freedom to the whole world. The Czechoslovak events of the thirties aroused in him angry protest (*Zpěvy nenávisti*) against the reactionary forces within and outside Czechoslovakia and once more brought

8. F. Kudeříková, *Zlomek života* (Prague, 1961), p. 136.

9. L. Špačková, *Takový byl* (Prague, 1957), pp. 59, 60.

him closer to the political issues. In reading his comments on them, whether in poetry or prose, one might think that with the exception of the working class Czechoslovakia was disposed to conform to fascism rather than to accept communism. In 1937 Neumann published *Anti-Gide*, an answer to Gide's negative criticism of Soviet Russia. Neumann's poetry of that time dealt with such "historical reality" (*istoricheskaia konkretnost'*) as the civil war in Spain, the Negroes in Scottsboro, the Nazis, and the Russian five-year plan. This was soapbox oratory, described properly as propaganda poetry (*agitatsionnaia poeziia*), although on account of it Neumann was named the father of "socialist-realist" poetry.

There was only one situation in which Neumann seemed oblivious of his Marxist weltanschauung, and this was in his beloved pastoral. His worship of it found its best poetic expression in his *Kniha lesů, vod a strání* [The book of woods, waters and slopes, 1917], the book by which he will most probably be remembered as a poet. He, on his part, underrated this work and did not like at all the remark of one of his critics who compared it with the pastoral verse of Vítězslav Hálek.[10] In the twenties, when Karel Čapek was translating Apollinaire's and Cendrars' poetry, Hálek's verse was considered to be sentimental and the very opposite of the contemporary idea of what poetry should be, hence Neumann's chagrin. His diary, *Československá cesta* (1933), kept during a hiking expedition in Carpatho-Russia, records his lifelong belief in the values of the pastoral and his hatred of those who invade it with their hotels and cars. His hatred is usually expressed in crude clichés; his love for nature, on the other hand, always has the ring of authenticity.

The metaphoric prophesy, "Bělostně kvetoucí třešně, rostoucí pro rudé ovoce . . . ,"[11] proved to be a socialist reality; the cherry trees of Czechoslovakia were to bear fruit for the communist society, as the poet had wished it. His militant partisanship

10. Ibid., p. 53.

11. S. K. Neumann, *Československá cesta* (Prague, 1952), p. 332.

and his progressive attitude were rewarded in 1945 with the title of National Artist. The late president Klement Gottwald spoke of him as "our greatest and most courageous poet"; the Czech Stalinist critic Ladislav Štoll praised his work as "the pillar of Czech poetry" for the preceding fifty years and eulogized his "socialist orientation, his adherence to the Communist party, to the Soviet Union, to Lenin and Stalin."[12]

Like Neumann and Majerová, Olbracht was one of the first Czech writers to enter the Communist party. His biographical records tells us that he read the Communist Manifesto while he was still in his teens. He left his studies and went to Vienna, where he worked for the social democratic periodical *Dělnické listy*. Like many of the Czech intellectuals of those years (1909–16), he was an "anarchist" and his socialist orientation was already obvious in his early writing. In 1908 he wrote about "socialist poetry";[13] in 1913, reviewing Gorki's play *Na dne* (*The Lower Depths*), he called it "socialist drama," and in his review discussed "new literature" as incompatible with the old and with a great future ahead. The Russian history of Czech literature gives the Russian October Revolution as a milestone in Olbracht's life and work. There is some truth in it. In 1919 Olbracht wrote in the Social Democratic Prague daily *Právo lidu* that Russia gave birth to a new world and a new culture. However, with the exception of *Anna, proletářka* [Anna, the proletarian, 1928], his fiction does not reflect his political ideas, at least not as closely as does Majerová's. His novels and short stories published before World War I are typical of the Czech fiction of that period and do not transmit directly their author's socialist ideology. In the 1953 edition of his novel *Podivné přátelství herce Jesenia* [The strange friendship of the actor Jesenius, 1918], Olbracht felt it necessary to apologize for his hero, who was too much of an individualist and, though socialist minded, lacked

12. L. Štoll, *Třicet let bojů za českou socialistickou poesii* (Prague, 1950), pp. 17, 18.

13. I. Olbracht, *O umění a společnosti* (Prague, 1958), pp. 14, 16.

the true Marxist perspective. The official Russian literary history expressed similar reservations.[14] Moreover, Olbracht's two best works, *Nikola Šuhaj* [Nikola Šuhaj, robber, 1933] and *Golet v údolí* [The bitter and the sweet, 1937], considered by many to be the masterpieces of modern Czech prose, depend but vaguely on socialist realism. Nevertheless, the Marxist critics interpreted *Nikola Šuhaj* as a protest "zakarpatskovo naroda protiv voiny i ugnetatelei" (of the Carpatho-Russian nation against war and oppression).[15] On the other hand, it is surprising that Russian criticism did not introduce into the discussion the Slovak folklore hero Janošík, who is so obviously connected with the hero of Olbracht's novel. *Golet v údolí*, a collection of stories about the Carpatho-Russian Jewry, is narrated with ethnographical realism, delightful humor, and much originality. For the Russians, *Golet v údolí* and to a certain extent also *Nikola Šuhaj*, have a minor significance, at least in comparison with *Anna, proletářka*, the novel about "the revolutionary year 1920," as Olbracht himself called it in the 1950 edition.

Anna, the proletarian, served as a maid in a degenerate bourgeois family; her lover, later her husband, was a class-conscious worker and a member of the Social Democratic party, and Anna followed in his footsteps. At the end of the novel we find Anna in the forefront of the workers' revolt. The revolt is historical, as is the entire political aspect of Anna's story. It records the meetings in Lidový Dům on Hybernská Ulice and the evenings organized by the club Karel Marx; it documents the split between the right and left wing of the Social Democratic party, which was "80 percent Communist" at that time;[16] and political personalities of the Czech twenties—J. Šmeral, G. Haberman, J. Stivín—appear in it. Olbracht wrote the novel as a close witness of this period, and it may be that in the future *Anna, proletářka* will be read precisely because of it. "We fought against

14. *Ocherki*, p. 478. 15. Ibid., p. 485.

16. Olbracht, *Anna proletářka* (Prague, 1950), p. 262.

the agrarian party, against big industry, banking, business, against the rightist elements . . . in short against the bourgeois democracy," recalled Olbracht in the foreword to *Anna, proletářka.* In Russia the novel was hailed as one of the first achievements of socialist realism outside the Soviet Union; it was translated into Russian, Ukrainian, German, and Japanese.

Socialist realism as represented by Olbracht, Majerová, and Neumann consisted chiefly in support of Marxism: they attacked more or less directly the decadent capitalist world and extolled the invincible forces of communism. Yet both Olbracht and Neumann also wrote fiction and poetry which had little or no relationship to socialist realism. Slovakia had a writer who approximated the new Russian model of socialist realism better than any of his older Slovak or Czech contemporaries. He was Petr Jilemnický, a Czech by birth who adopted Slovakia, its literature, and language as his own. With Fučík, Neumann, and Václavek, he is considered to be an exponent of the Communist cause in Czechoslovakia.

When Jilemnický was writing his first experiments in prose, the cry of the day was futurism and constructivism. Following the literary vogue, Jilemnický chose exotic motifs like the Ku Klux Klan in the United States or colonialism in Africa. His first publication in book form, *Devadesát devět bílých koní* [Ninety-nine white horses, 1921], was illustrated by J. Štýrský, later the representative of Czech surrealism. At that time Jilemnický was teaching in a small village, and the avant-garde news from Prague cafés lost its glamour before it could reach him. Nevertheless, for some time Jilemnický remained attracted by Devětsil, the avant-garde group destined to enter literary history; but his contact with Gottwald, the future president of Czechoslovakia, turned out to be more significant than his first literary affiliations. In 1924 Gottwald was canvassing and propagandizing in the region of Baňská Bystrica, where Jilemnický was doing his military service, and the two men met. Jilemnický, who entered the Communist party in 1922, was active in organizing the local youth and writing for the Slovak Communist press. After he had left the army, he decided to stay in Slovakia. From then on his life was identified with the party, with the proletarian of the Slovak village and with the Slovak literature. In 1926, Jilemnický left with a group of five hundred workers, peasants, and craftsmen for Frunze in Karakirgizia. The enterprise was called Interhelpo and Jilemnický's part in it gave it a literary reputation. His novel *Zuniaci krok* [A resounding step, 1930], based on his experience in the Caucasian village Krasno-Chekhovka, has been compared to the Russian novels *Podniataia tselina* [Virgin soil upturned, 1937] by M. A. Sholokhov and *Bruski* [Brusski, 1928–37] by F. I. Panferov. The next step and the next stage in Jilemnický's socialist education was the Institute of Journalism (Gosudarstvennyi institut zhurnalistiki) in Moscow. It was there that his Marxism received its final touch.

Jilemnický believed that literature should and must serve the proletarian cause. At the Congress of Soviet Writers in 1934, together with Václavek and Fučík, Jilemnický stood in the loyal camp while Teige and the Slovak Novomeský sided with the deviators. Today the literary portraits of the participants of the congress might be read as political history; their personal lives were determined by its march whether they were Pasternak or Jilemnický, Nezval or Novomeský. Jilemnický's major novel, *Pole neoraná* [Unploughed fields, 1932], was written under the impact of the Czechoslovak economic crisis and its unemployment, which put a new burden on the Slovak proletarian. The hero of the novel is an agricultural proletarian who joins the class-conscious workers because he realizes that a better life may be achieved only through the collective effort of all proletarians. On 25 November 1932 Gottwald gave a fiery speech in the Czechoslovak parliament, in which he denounced the Czech capitalists for bringing starvation and death upon the Slovak village.[17] The whole speech could be interpreted as the subject for Jilemnický's novel *Kus cukru* [A piece of sugar, 1934]. Jilem-

17. K. Gottwald, *Spisy*, 15 vols. (Prague, 1951–53) 4:119–30.

nický followed the party line but also wrote with his own statistics at hand: in his school only four of sixty-nine children had their own beds and only twelve lived in a house which had more than one room. He summed up the message of his *Kus cukru:* everyone has the right to taste the honey.[18] It is revealing to compare Jilemnický's portrayal of the Slovak peasant with Čapek's. The comparison tells both about the authors and about the crisis of the Czechoslovak thirties. At that time Čapek came to the Slovak village as a visitor, whereas Jilemnický lived there for years in daily contact with its people. Čapek scouted the landscape for his novel *Hordubal* and used secondhand ethnographical information; everything else was literature. Determined by psychological and even "detective" elements, the novel proposed a relativist concept of a "murder" story. In *Víťazný pád* [Glorious fall, 1929] and also in *Návrat* [The return, 1930], Jilemnický treated a similar situation. In *Hordubal* the adultery ended in murder, in *Návrat* the adulteress was forgiven; this meant not merely another possible solution but also another value-motivation. Jilemnický made the husband merciful because the woman sinned, crushed by the society surrounding her. Čapek saw his peasant as an injured man; Jilemnický saw him determined by his social condition. Čapek wrote about an individual murder case; Jilemnický about the economic situation. Čapek's jury could not see clearly who committed the crime; Jilemnický's jurors (*Víťazný pád*) set the murderer free because they found that society was guilty. Hordubal's wife sinned out of sheer sensuality, whereas the heroine of *Návrat* was pushed to unfaithfulness by desperate poverty. Čapek wrote a relativist-humanist novel about a *crime passionel*, while Jilemnický presented the social-economic pattern of a poverty-stricken Slovak village.

When in 1938 Hlinka's regime took over in Slovakia, Jilemnický was obliged to leave. For a short while he settled in the Czech town of Litomyšl, but in 1942 he was arrested and im-

18. Břetislav Truhlář, *Petr Jilemnický* (Prague, 1959), p. 64.

prisoned, first in the Czech Terezín and then in the German concentration camp Griebo. After the end of the war he returned to his country by adoption, Slovakia. He assumed official duties, the last of which was in Moscow where he went as cultural attaché (1948). He was honored with the title of National Artist only posthumously.

In spite of his many postwar activities, Jilemnický succeeded in writing *Kronika* [Chronicle, 1945], a novel about the Slovak uprising. Once more Jilemnický chose as his locale the Slovak village, its mountains haunted by Slovak partisans and Russian parachutists and raided by the Germans. By 1960, *Kronika* went to eight Slovak and six Czech editions. With an introduction by B. Polevoi, it was published in Moscow in 1948 and again by Nakladateľstvo cudzoiazychnii literatury (publishing house for literature in translation) in 1952. *Kus cukru* had two Russian editions, one in 1950 and a second in 1951. Jilemnický's short stories ("Návrat" among them) were also published in 1953 and 1956.

One of the distinguished writers favored by the Russians is Marie Pujmanová (1893–1956). The Russians are interested in her work not merely because of her communist orientation—she was a *borets*, a fighter for socialism—but also because of the literary qualities of her work. Born into a family of the upper-middle class, she was a convert to Marxism. Her enthusiastic partisanship and her talent made up for the past. The Marxist critics do not try to hide her bourgeois background, although they describe it with caution. She was a valuable acquisition for the Communists, especially since the last war, when their writers' ranks were thinned either by natural death or by Nazi terror. Pujmanová responded fully to the expectation of the party.

The subject of her first novel, her home and family world, to which she returned again and again, survived in her socialist period and in her major works. All Pujmanová's young people were created from one easily recognized mold: the world of her childhood and adolescence as she portrayed it first in *Pod křídly*

[Under the wings, 1917]. The adults of the outside world, on the other hand, were created from observation and reasoning. Such is, for example, the character in her "Měšťačka" [A bourgeois]. This vignette, one of her first printed stories (in *Kmen*, 1917), is never forgotten by her Marxist critics. It is surprising that Pujmanová could give such a shallow portrayal of the class to which she herself belonged. She would judge the doom of the bourgeoisie by a mere glance at the beach or swimming pool; there the bourgeois is seen in all the ugliness of his or her obesity. For Pujmanová, as for the cartoonist, obesity was a class phenomenon.

Other early writings of Pujmanová show her unusual talent but do not predict her later socialist-realist orientation. It did not come overnight. In 1932 she took part in the expedition of Czechoslovak leftist writers to Most where the miners were on strike. It was then that Pujmanová met Fučík. This group of writers also planned a visit to the textile factories in the north of Bohemia. These activities and contacts with people like Fučík familiarized Pujmanová with certain politico-literary aspects of communism and steered her toward socialist realism. In the summer of 1932 she visited Soviet Russia, learned Russian, and read Gorki and Maiakovskii in the original—in the last part of her *Trilogy* one of her heroines quotes *Levyi marsh* [Left march]. Pujmanová herself described her visit to Russia as a turning point of her career. After she returned, she started to publish in the Communist press (*Levá fronta* and *Tvorba* for example) and after 1937 also wrote for *Rudé právo*, the Communist daily. Still, she was not a member of the party. B. Václavek, the main exponent of the theory of socialist realism in Czechoslovakia, was the man whom Pujmanová approached when she wanted to study textile factories for her novel *Lidé na křižovatce* [People at the crossroads, 1937]. Like Svatopluk (*Botostroj*) she wrote about Baťa and Zlín, though she changed the shoe factory into a textile factory and the town's name into Úly. Not everything in *Lidé na křižovatce* was socialist realism; it still reflected the "sheltered world" of her *Pod křídly;* nevertheless it was a clear step in the direction of socialist realism.

In a way communism and its literary theory helped Pujmanová overcome a creative crisis which followed her first success. She had an exceptional gift of observation and sensitivity; yet her talent was not of the caliber to create an independent vision of the world. Socialist realism offered her a solution, a backbone for her fiction. In the collection of poetry *Praha* (1954), she confessed her dependence on the party: "I was an unhappy and unstable creature . . . before I met you my comrades. . . . What would I be without you?—an aging woman."[19] When *Lidé na křižovatce* was published, the periodical *Kritický měsíčník*[20] reviewed it with reservation; S. K. Neumann and B. Václavek, on the contrary, praised it as a new and important achievement of Czech socialist realism. S. K. Neumann, in *Tvorba*, placed Pujmanová ahead of her contemporaries, Olbracht included.[21]

In 1946 the Congress of Czechoslovak Writers proclaimed the involvement of literature in the national life and President Beneš pleaded in vain for "literature above parties and classes." Pujmanová then stood in the very foreground of government-issued and government-approved literature. She held no official position, but still she enjoyed an authority and voiced it, using more and more the official terminology. She identified herself with the party and its goals: "Má vlasti, dávno splynula's mně s Stranou . . ." (from the poem *Má strano života* in *Praha*). Her work, her fiction and travelogues, were translated into Russian, and she contributed to such Russian literary magazines as *Literaturnaia gazeta.* The two remaining parts of her trilogy[22] were published with éclat. In terms of history the second book *Hra s ohněm* [Playing with fire], is the story of the Reichstag fire and

19. From the poem *Loučím se s Tebou,* in *Praha* (Prague, 1954).

20. *Kritický měsíčník,* 1938, pp. 39–42.

21. S. K. Neumann, *Umění a politika,* 2 vols. (Prague, 1953) 1:197–99.

22. *Lidé na křižovatce,* 1937; *Hra s ohněm,* 1948; *Život proti smrti,* 1952.

the trial of Dimitrov seen through the eyes of a Czech Communist lawyer. The Russian critic Bernshtein praises her for avoiding reportage and documentary style and for her command of the multiple events (*potok sobytii*). He compares her novel with Sartre's *Les Chemins de la liberté* (part 2, "Les Sursis"). The comparison favors Pujmanová because in Bernshtein's opinion she avoided the disintegration of the story (*rozpad obraza*), which he believes to be a defect of Sartre's novel. Bernshtein also emphasized the optimism of her heroes and the role assigned to Communists in the development of her fictional history; further he underlined her presentation of the liberation of Czechoslovakia by the Red Army, which was glorified in the title of the third work, *Život proti smrti* [Life against death]—the Soviet Union is life (*život*) and Nazi Germany death (*smrt*).

L. T. Motyleva[23] paid Pujmanová a compliment when she associated her trilogy with the Tolstoyan tradition—"tolstovskaia traditsiia." Pujmanová herself confessed her admiration for the Russian classic; she compared the fall of Napoleon with the fall of Hitler, and added that such was the end of anyone "who dared to attack the Soviet Union."[24] The Czech critic J. Hájek had some reservations concerning Pujmanová's description of life in Soviet Gruzia (one of her protagonists went to Russia and worked there in a textile factory) and felt that her treatment of the Lidice tragedy and of life in concentration camps was based on secondhand information and therefore unconvincing. He described the trilogy as a work which had as its hero the whole Czech nation fighting by the side of the Soviet army, "the liberator of our country."[25]

This is not the place to discuss in detail the literary qualities of Pujmanová's work in general and of her trilogy in particular.

23. T. L. Motyleva, *O mirovom znachenii L. N. Tolstovo*, Moscow, 1957, pp. 694–707.

24. Ibid., p. 695.

25. J. Hájek, *Literatura a život* (Prague, 1955), p. 116.

Nevertheless, the English reader should be introduced to at least one of the major characters of the trilogy, Helena, since it is she who expresses with eloquence the author's views. She is the heroine who comes from the world of Pujmanová's children and adolescents. They all share one value: integrity, whether it be the integrity of sentiment, honor, or idea, and they all are ready to die for it. Helena dies for the idea of communism. She is a physician—a vocation symbolic of her dedication to the collective, a value which Pujmanová admires in Madame Curie, in physicians, or in Communists. The Russian critic Bernshtein described this very well. Helena dies as the victim of the Nazis. She is the female fictional counterpart of men like Julius Fučík. Helena's calvary and her last moments before the execution are described with ideological authenticity, yet without life-dimension. Fučík wrote his letters from prison expecting death; yet he did not write of facing the very last moments of his life and their uncommunicable experience.

In 1956 at the Congress of Czechoslovak Writers, Pujmanová spoke against the dissenters from the official literary line, called the opposition "hysterical," and even accused it of "revisionism."[26] This was indeed a long road from her impressionist beginnings under the guidance of R. Svobodová and from the time when F. X. Šalda started an article about one of her literary reviews with the words: "My young and beautiful friend Mrs. Pujmanová-Hennerová. . . ."[27] It was even a long way from the first part of her trilogy.

There were other less prominent representatives of Czechoslovak socialist realism known also to the Russians. Among the most often cited were G. Včelička (*Kavárna na hlavní třídě* [The café on Main Street], 1932), V. Řezáč (*Bitva* [The battle], 1954), T. Svatopluk (*Botostroj*, 1933), J. Káňa (*Válkou narušení* [Touched by war], 1951), and J. Weiss (*Volání o pomoc* [A call

26. *Literární noviny*, 1956, no. 21.

27. F. X. Šalda, *Soubor díla F. X. Šaldy*, 22 vols. (Prague 1948–59), 20:240.

for help], 1959). Včelička's novel attacked the exploitation of employees in a Prague café; Svatopluk the capitalist system as it existed in Baťa's Zlín. Weiss wrote about the Nazi persecution of Jews, Káňa about the Prague proletarian youth of World War I, Řezáč about the socialist community in the former Sudetenland. In one form or another, they all adhered to the pattern of socialist realism. With the second half of our century, however, socialist realism lost its interest for young writers who, born during the thirties and remembering the last war as their childhood, grew out of the theory of socialist realism; for them, the evils of the capitalist society were a matter of the past. "Optimistic" motifs like building a factory or shock-work seemed unrealistic and were soon looked upon as disgraceful. The party would certainly love to see the writers devote their efforts to propaganda and to reform of the rebellious young people. Yet the best of the writers, even if they are Communists and party men, remain unresponsive to its demands. The young people love jazz, and Majerová had no chance to win them over to the polka (*Ševcovská polka a jiné radosti* [The cobbler's polka]). Her model of socialist realism is simply outdated; the coal mines are socialized, and those who did not know life in capitalist countries are not equipped to appreciate the blessings of socialism. S. K. Neumann's oratory, which had the power to inspire courage in Nazi victims, also lost a great part of its luster; it exists as poetry, not as "socialist realist poetry." In Slovakia the subject of the Slovak uprising is very much alive; but its story, which after 1945–48 yielded model socialist realism, in the sixties served as an argument for the protest against "the cult of the personality."

# 6
# THE NEW "WECHSELSEITIGKEIT"

SHOULD Jan Kollár (1793–1852) be able to witness the contemporary Slavic world he would be amazed at how completely his great dream of a Slavic cultural exchange, which he called *Wechselseitigkeit,* had come true. All, or nearly all his proposals were realized, though with changes which always occur during the realization of an idea. At first, Kollár would perhaps be puzzled to see that the Slavic heaven—he imagined such a Slavic *Paradiso* in his *Slávy dcera*—had been opened to the archenemies of the Slavs, the Germans, and the Hungarians. Other facts, however, should put him at ease: the book catalog published in Slovakia, for example, where he could see the recently issued *Slovatskaia literatura* [Slovak literature] (Turčianský sv. Martin, 1965). He might also be offered other publications in Russian, by the Russians and for the Russians, and all of them dedicated to Czech and Slovak literature. He could not but be convinced that the Slavic *Wechselseitigkeit* had been established. One of its major literary events was the publication of *Ocherki istorii cheshskoi literatury XIX–XX vekov* (Moscow, 1963), a close parallel to the Czech *Dějiny české literatury.*[1] The Russian work

1. [History of Czech literature] (Prague, 1959–61); henceforth *Dějiny.*

is more than an expression of cultural exchange; it is a scholarly achievement of its own and has no comparable publication outside Czechoslovakia.

The spirit of the new Slavic *Wechselseitigkeit* centers in the Academies, the authorities on which scholars depend directly or indirectly; literary scholarship could hardly live outside their walls. Independent literary history or criticism has some chance of appearing in periodicals; however this involves personal risks for the author and for the editor. Literary criticism reduced to the page of an introduction or afterword must also follow the policy of the Academies. The Czech *Dějiny* and the Russian *Ocherki* are projects of their respective Academies and display a striking resemblance in size of volumes, arrangement of essays, and in the uniform concept of the periodicity of Czech literature. Each section is headed by an article which outlines the character of the period in question and its writers, the most important of whom are distinguished by one-chapter monographs. The whole publication is the work of the collective and written by specialists in the field. It seems noteworthy that *Ocherki* quotes Czech poets in good and often very good translations; it proves how much genuine interest the Russian poets and translators bring to Czech poetry. The poet Kollár would be delighted. His "Slavic" sentiment and his poet's pride would be flattered if he were able to finger through the three-volume *Antologiia cheshskoi poezii* [Anthology of Czech poetry] (Moscow, 1959). For he would find there the introduction to his *Slávy dcera*, its sonnets, and the proof of the accuracy of his judgment: the Russian and the Czech languages are but two "dialects." Otherwise his sonnet 225 would not sound as well in Russian as it does:

*Gordyi Kreml' siiai! Moskva sviataia!*
*S zolotymi bashniami stena!*

In its entirety, the anthology is not only the most impressive but also the best existing collection of translated Czech poetry. It covers the history of modern Czech verse, beginning with

Václav Thám (1765–1816), the dedicated patriot of the Czech literary renaissance, and concludes with contemporary poets. The linguistic and cultural affinities of Russian and Czech brought marvelous results, particularly where the verse derived its metrics and mood from folksong—as in, for example, Erben's *Vodník* (in Russian *Vodnianoi* [The water-sprite]). The anthology avoids the usual pitfalls of anthologies because it does not limit itself to samples or essential readings but gives generous space to every important poet. The ideological bias is felt mostly in volume 3, headed by S. K. Neumann's *Blagodarnost' sovetskomu svazu* [Thanksgiving to Soviet Russia]. In this part of the anthology the favorites distinguish themselves by the number of pages allocated to them. Seifert, whose place is second only to Nezval, has twenty-four pages, while Hora has twenty-nine. Nezval the invincible has fifty-two, and included there of course is the poem *Odevzdal jsem svůj lístek revoluci* (the Russian title is *Za revoliutsiiu ia otdal golos svoi* [I voted for revolution]). The national classics, especially Kollár, fared very well. The author of *Slávy dcera* would be moved; the introduction to it was translated in its original hexameter: "Vizhu rodnuiu stranu—i slezy iz glaz moikh liutsia."

There is one small but revealing detail shared by both *Dějiny* and *Ocherki:* they never tire of citing and quoting Z. Nejedlý and J. Fučík, and frequently for no other reason than propaganda. Of course Nejedlý, as well as being a party man of long standing, was a scholar; Fučík, on the other hand, was a young journalist who in addition to his obligations to the party also wrote literary criticism. Even if one should consider Nejedlý's and Fučík's contributions to literature important, the redundant citations and quotations from them are too conspicuous not to provoke doubts about their pertinence. The major difference between *Ocherki* and *Dějiny* is the range of their subject matter. *Dějiny* in three volumes of about two thousand pages covers the medieval period and discusses in detail the seventeenth and eighteenth centuries, while the single volume of *Ocherki* is limited to the modern part of Czech literature. *Dějiny* is an imposing work and outdoes the previous and comparable publications in the scope of collective scholarship, but its monolithic ideology, though expected, has an odd effect particularly when applied to the beginnings of Slavic literacy.

According to *Dějiny*, the Cyril and Methodius Moravian mission had as its goal the strengthening of the local priesthood and its ally, the secular power (*D.* 1:32).[2] The contemporary archeological findings in Velká Morava, Staré město, Mokrá u Velehradu, and Mikulčice "testify to the class character of Christianity" (*D.* 1:32). This controversial statement is followed, however, by useful and reliable information about *Proglas*, the verse introduction to the translation of the Gospel into Church Slavonic. About the Czech dux Boleslav II (967–999), *Dějiny* informs us that he founded "centers of ideological propaganda in the new churches" (*D.* 1:50). Further, the otherwise competent chapter about the twelfth-century chronicler Cosmas Pragensis is interspersed with dicta like "he [Cosmas] did not disdain the people [*nepřezíral lid*]" or "he glorified the creative forces of the people unprotected by law" (*D.* 1:74, 75). Sometimes the rigid adherence to the Marxist tenets may force awkward formulations upon the scholar. In the pages dealing with "Život sv. Kateřiny" [The life of Saint Catherine] the writer tells us that the fourteenth-century legend "had no bearing on the problems affecting the life of the people" and sees in the saint's Thomist dispute with the pagan sages an "antidemocratic" attitude. He concedes that the passage about the martyrdom of the saint belongs to "the most beautiful poetry of our old literature" (*D.* 1:130, 131). On the other hand, *Dějiny* presents the early medieval Czech centuries, their ecclesiastical institutions, and activities in the convents and schools within the framework of their contemporary material and economic culture, much in the same manner as the medievalists of the West. It is with the Czech fourteenth

2. References are to volume and page in *Dějiny* (*D.*), to page only in the one-volume *Ocherki* (*O.*).

and fifteenth centuries, and especially with the Hussite movement, that *Dějiny* intones a strong ideological pathos.

Every Czech is at home with the idea of Hussitism; the idea is popular and of long standing. Starting with the historian F. Palacký (1798–1876), it runs like a red thread throughout Czech intellectual history. Even a heroine (or hero) of a Czech decadent novel might dabble with a reference to this period. An intellectual Czech liberal and the man in the street would be in agreement that the Hussite period belonged to the most glorious and admirable exploits of Czech past. *Dějiny* headed the part dedicated to the literature of that time with the eloquent title "Zlidovění literatury v době husitské" [The democratization of literature in the Hussite period]. That Jan Hus was a priest involved in the theological questions of his time and concerned with the reform of religious life remained quite secondary and as if unimportant. He is portrayed as the spokesman of the people, the leader of the people who let himself be guided by the people. It was from this relationship that his "progressive actions" took their vigor (*D.* 1:197). He and the Czech nation were victims of the ecclesiastic and secular reactionary forces both inside and outside Bohemia. Special attention was given by *Dějiny* to the Hussite song, an "ideological weapon of the people" (*D.* 1:242). To a great extent the popularity of the Hussite song is due to Z. Nejedlý and his major work *Dějiny husitského zpěvu* [History of the Hussite song].

The Czech concept of Hussitism was taken over by *Ocherki.* The Russian Marxist tradition concerning this period goes back to Karl Marx, who was aware of the Hussite impact on the Czech mind, as is evident from his letters to Engels and also from his notes. *Ocherki*, dealing with Hus and his time, introduces him as the defender of "truth" and "justice"; for *Ocherki* it is important that Hus "revolted against the Church" and that the Hussite warriors opposed the "feudal European reaction," including the Pope and the Hungarians. The bibliography for this part of Czech literature, as given by *Dějiny*, is complete and up to date and includes standard works like those of Curtius or Dreves. The ideological guidance was reserved for *Istoriia filosofii* [History of philosophy] (Moscow, 1940–41), particularly its first volume *Filosofiia antichnovo i feodalňovo obshchestva* [Philosophy of the ancient and medieval world], translated into Czech in 1950–52. Also *Istoriia srednikh vekov* [Medieval history], published by the Institute of History of the Russian Academy and translated into Czech in 1957–58, must be considered a guide.

"The Hussite road toward the democratization of the culture was obstructed by the Counter-Reformation"—with these words *Dějiny* opens its chapter on the baroque period. Anyone with the slightest knowledge of Marxism can guess its approach to baroque. In contrast to the Hussite period, it was traditionally viewed by the Czechs as a period of literary decadence. The Russians accepted the Czech approach wholeheartedly; it suited their historical aversion to Catholicism and fitted their atheistic outlook. The Russians seem to have remained untouched by the European vogue of baroque music and art, which strongly influenced the recent Czech evaluation of this period. In contemporary Czechoslovakia, baroque art and music have high currency, the government restores baroque monuments and keeps up its churches, without encouraging their services of course. To a degree, *Dějiny*'s interpretation of the baroque literature shares in this trend which started in the thirties, but the ideological coating is new; it tells that the masses resisted the official Counter-Reformation propaganda and that the class struggle continued in the form of religious strife (*D.* 1:384, 386). The memory of the Hussite past manifested itself in revolts and heresy and lived in songs, prophesies, and folktales (*D.* 1:386). The period was not one of utter darkness as it was labeled by some scholars; the people's resistance to the pressures of the reactionary forces, both ecclesiastic and secular, must be appraised. Between the people and their masters "raged a merciless class struggle"—*zuřil nelítostný třídní boj* (*D.* 1:386). In the flow of the ideological oratory, concessions are made—Jungmann had already made them—for the Czech baroque architecture "worthy of our admiration" (*D.* 1:387). Still, one is reminded that the baroque effects are "grotesque" and "ridiculous," and that it is the "content" of the work of art and not its "form" which really matters. The literary period of the Czech baroque and its later mannerist stage, rococo, is traditionally dated by the years 1650–1780. With its conclusion—and in this all the Czech literary historians agree—there was little left which could compare to the literary achievements of other European countries. The baroque cultural pattern lived in Bohemia as art and music; as literature it reached its low ebb. The development which grew out of this cultural depression is called *doba obrozenská*—the period of literary renaissance. At this point the Marxist literary historian, Czech or Russian, takes off from the familiar grounds and applies his theory of literature with confidence, for he advances through the decades of the century which gave rise to his own weltanschauung.

The traditional interpretation of the Czech *obrození*, also called the Czech Enlightenment, recognized its dependence on the European Age of Reason. The foremost author and scholar of this time, Josef Jungmann (1773–1847), translated Milton's *Paradise Lost* in 1811–18, and this literary work was considered to be the cornerstone of modern Czech poetry, not only by the literary historians but by the poets themselves, Vrchlický to name one. This fact is (and must be) minimized by the Marxist critic, since it forewarns against the "overestimation" of foreign influence and points out that the Western literary impact on Czech literature always brought with it the danger of cosmopolitanism, whereas the Russian influence returned the Czech mind to its "true" national character (*D.* 2:9). Both *Dějiny* and *Ocherki* refuse to view the Czech Enlightenment in the perspective of the French eighteenth century and of German Romanticism; for them this period has a predominantly *lidový* (people's) character and should be interpreted as the protest of the Czech patriots against the feudal order. The Romantic sentiment is viewed as the cradle of revolt, and the Romantic despair as the outcome of the isolation enforced on the poet by the society. The period's interest in folklore has to be understood and interpreted against the backdrop of the social changes appearing with the rise of capitalism (*D.* 2:7, 147). The influence of Herder, the brothers Grimm, and still others is reduced to bare names.

The industrial revolution established the lands of the Czech crown as important partners in the economy of the Austrian monarchy, and the Czech politico-cultural aims were strengthened accordingly. The year 1848 found the Czechs on the alert. The immediate results of the Prague uprising were disastrous; yet it was obvious that Czech literature, which had a lion's share in bringing on the Czech actions, would live and give its full support to the national demands. For the Marxist literary historian, the year 1848 is an ever-present sign on his mind's horizon; it forecasts revolution, socialism, and progress. From the milestone 1848 *Dějiny* and *Ocherki* proceed with smooth eloquence. The authors are divided roughly into two groups "progressive" and "reactionary," and the art of the critic consists in working out the necessary nuances. That these often have to be stretched on a procrustean bed should not surprise anyone. It may happen that "revolutionary" characteristics are attributed to a writer in whom one would never look for them. This, however, the Marxist critic would say is caused by the blindness of the bourgeois mind.

Nevertheless, there are instances where the "reactionary" and the Marxist critic see eye to eye and thus support the idea that literary criticism is literary criticism in spite of ideological barriers. *Ocherki*, for example, says about Neumann's *Rudé zpěvy* [Red songs, 1923]: "His poetry conveyed the powerful revolutionary drive in Czechoslovakia" (*O.* 367), and Arne Novák, the prewar "reactionary" critic, describes the same collection as "the adamant stand of a Communist soldier." About Seifert's early collection of poetry (1920), Arne Novák says that it is "a confession of a revolutionary proletarian dazed by the idea of revolution," while *Ocherki* expresses the same thought with the words: "He hated the situation around him; he knew how necessary the revolution was" (*O.* 370). *Ocherki* characterizes *Pekař Marhoul* [The baker Marhoul, 1924], the major work of V. Vančura, as "the story of a good man living in the capitalist jungle," and Arne Novák has it as "the hard struggle of a proletarian for his bread." On the other hand, Novák does not even list Jiří Hausmann, who was, *Ocherki* assures us, a "talantnyi satirik" and who wrote satires on the political personalities of the Right: Kramář, Rašín, Dyk, and Machar. One wonders whether *Ocherki* would revive Hausmann's satire so readily if it had been directed against the Left. Similarly, Antonín Marek (1872–1923), who is barely mentioned in Novák's standard textbook, has a sizable place in *Ocherki;* is it because, originally a carpenter and later a journalist, he was "a true proletarian poet" who had the merit of translating the *International* into Czech? *Ocherki* accused Medek—one of the leading personalities of the Czechoslovak Legions in World War I—of falsifying (*izvratil*) history in his novels about the Czech army in Russia. Medek was charged with misunderstanding the meaning of the Russian October Revolution (*on neponial' smysl Oktiabra*), another of the current criteria used both by *Ocherki* and *Dějiny.* In some cases political measures were applied with less transparency. Božena Benešová (1873–1936) was blamed for promoting the idea of "Czechoslovakia born from the resistance against the Central Powers." The Communist regime removed the twenty-eighth of October, 1918, from the memorable days of the Czechoslovak calendar and evidently also rejected the fiction dealing with this date in any positive way. *Ocherki* appears to be especially intransigent in this respect.

The more *Dějiny* and *Ocherki* advance in our century, the more they are on the politico-ideological offensive. In the early twenties, the center of the "new revolutionary culture" was *Proletkult*, the publishing arm of the Czechoslovak Communist party, with the old combatant S. K. Neumann as its secretary. *Prolet-*

*kult* published Russian poems in Czech—*Glavnaia ulitsa* [The main Street] by D. Bednyi, *Levyi marsh* [Left march] by Maiakovskii, and *Dvenadsat'* [The twelve] by Blok. The magazine *Kmen*, of which S. K. Neumann was editor, was also the domain of the left-oriented literature. Neumann's major contribution to the avant-garde of the twenties was the magazine *Červen*, which will be remembered because for a time it succeeded in grouping intellectuals, poets, authors, and artists who were to represent the generation of the First Czechoslovak Republic. *Červen* published the translation of an article by Lenin and texts signed by Josef and Karel Čapek, Vítězslav Nezval, Jaroslav Seifert, and Vladislav Vančura. Later the group dispersed although a number of *Červen*'s original contributors continued to have close ties with the party.

During the twenties, the word *revolution* sounded with ebullience in the verse of S. K. Neumann, J. Hora, J. Wolker, V. Nezval, J. Seifert, and still others. Hardly any of the foremost poets of the period are missing in the collective homage to Soviet Russia *SSSR v československé poesii* [USSR in Czech poetry, 1936]. The value of their poems varies; yet many are more than mere incidental poetry. One cannot leave unnoticed Seifert's *Město Leninovo* [The city of Lenin] and its stanza

*Bývalý palác admirality*
*empirová lastura, z které se narodila Venuše*
*s námořní čapkou.*
*Byl to malý zázrak.*
*Toť vše.*

("The palace, once of the Admiralty / the Empire shell from which Venus was born / she wore a sailor's cap. / A small miracle indeed. / That was all.") Nor can anyone overlook S. K. Neumann's *Poděkování Sovětskému svazu*, cited and quoted by the whole generation of Czechoslovak Communists.

From 1925 on the events allow *Dějiny* and *Ocherki* to apply the tenets of Marxist literary criticism even more rigorously.

The tenets should not be viewed as something artificially grafted on the trunk of Czechoslovak literature. The Stalinist policy was new and coercive; its ideas were not, at least not entirely. They had been proposed and accepted before in the very midst of the Czechoslovak democracy. In 1936, the well-known critic A. M. Píša wrote *Proletářská poesie* [Proletarian poetry], in which—not unlike *Dějiny* and *Ocherki*—he traced the "socialist-proletarian" element of Czech literature back to the Czech Vormärz period, to the year 1848, and to the "progressive tendencies" of the last century. He recorded their presence in the Hugolian humanism of Vrchlický and in the social themes of Sládek and especially of Sv. Čech. He cited Machar, Sova, and Bezruč, of course, as writers protesting against social injustice. And he singled out as truly proletarian the poets Neumann, Wolker, Seifert, Hora, and Hořejší. Píša identified the proletarian poet with the aftermath of World War I, with the radicalism of the masses, with the revolutionary drive, and with the Communist movement, which "was accepted by the majority of the literary youth."[3] This postwar generation saw in the war the condemnation of capitalism and bourgeoisie; its poets aspired to an active part in the class struggle, and professed revolutionary heroism and optimism; they opposed will and energy to individualism and religious passivity, and felt that technology should serve mankind instead of being misused by capitalism. Píša's language of 1937 is surprisingly contemporary. He claims that the proletarian poet was disappointed in the hoped-for freedom of the Czechoslovak Republic which he felt failed to bring "social freedom"; he segregated himself from the Czechoslovak democracy and from the Čapkian relativism.[4] Píša referred his readers to the periodicals *Kmen* and *Červen* as illustrative of "the knowledge and influence of the Russian Revolution in Czechoslovakia." With the exception of some formulations—Píša would, for example, use the

3. A. M. Píša, *Proletářská poesie* (Prague, 1936), p. 6.

4. Ibid., pp. 7–9.

word *zástupy* (crowds) where the Marxist critic might write *lid* (people) or *národ* (nation)—the Marxist concept of the "proletarian literature" existed already *in nuce* in Píša's essay of 1936.

The decade 1929–39 is set by *Dějiny* and *Ocherki* as the time of economic crisis and resistance to fascism. With the Czechoslovak Communist party as its leader, the progressive intellectuals mustered their forces for the conflict (*O.* 382). The Czech bourgeoisie sought to counteract the demands of the working class and lower its living standard, in other words, to obstruct and weaken the revolution. The Catholic writers—with J. Durych as their representative—were summed up as fascists, including the ruralist group close to the agrarian party and its press: J. Čep, K. Knap, and F. Křelina. Against this reactionary phalange stood the progressive fighters (*bortsy*, *bojovníci*), by which are meant those writers who took "pozitsii rabochevo klassa," that is, the socialist realists (*O.* 394). The ultimate criterion of an author's socialist realism, however, is determined by his political and not his literary action. In the sections of *Dějiny* and *Ocherki* dealing with the thirties, one encounters ideological evaluations in their crudest form. A reader without any other guidance than that of *Ocherki* must believe that Marie Majerová's fiction really reveals "depths [*glubiny*] of psychological insight" into the working class, and that Nejedlý and Fučík really were and remain unrivaled authorities of Czech literary criticism.

With the German occupation of Czechoslovakia (1939–45), it seems as if *Dějiny* and *Ocherki* abandoned altogether the field of literary history and literary criticism. It was not merely the pressure of ideology; the reason was in the events themselves: history took over and gave to the Communists and their party the decisive role in its development. With the historical 1945, *Dějiny* and *Ocherki* closed their surveys of modern Czech literature, an appropriate choice indeed. The authors who were to represent literature in the near future were born between the two world wars and were to make their debut or reputation only with the destalinization of Czech cultural affairs. In one of his short stories, Ivan Klíma, born in 1931, set this generation apart: "They say about us that we are the unfortunate generation. We learned something during thc war. We learned to eat dry bread, not to fear fatigue and suffering. We were cured of childhood and good faith. We witnessed many a vicious incident. The gestapo was coming to our houses, sometimes on the denunciation of a neighbor, and often we have read posters with names of people we knew well."[5]

5. Ivan Klíma, *Bezvadný den* (Prague, 1960), p. 178.

# 7

# CONCEPTUAL TERMINOLOGY

TO READ Marxist literary history and criticism well one should be acquainted with the repertoire of its terminology. Western literary criticism also has its linguistic mannerisms, used sometimes with elegance, sometimes with repetitious triteness. It would not be difficult to compile a list of words characteristic of our contemporary literary formulations. Nevertheless, the use of these terms is not compulsory; they are free for adoption or rejection. The Marxist critic, on the other hand, is tied by his particular code of literary communication. In this chapter an attempt will be made to examine some of its most salient and frequent terms.

At the head of our list, which is far from complete, must stand the word *lid* (people). This word is found time after time in any Czech or Slovak book about literature. Its meaning is not just "people" as ordinarily used; *lid* designates more than the passive recipients of a literary work, more than a mass composed of potential anonymous readers. The *lid* might accept or reject the literary work; it is a proteus that inspires the writer, yet might also appear as his judge. Literature has its very roots in the "people," and it is the "people's creativity" which is its ever-driving force, the individual author merely being an accidental executor. It is also suggested that any exclusion of the people's participation in literary affairs automatically causes a loss of values. Both the official *Dějiny* and *Ocherki* write of Tyl's plays and Jirásek's fiction that their heroes are not single individuals but "the Czech people." *Dějiny* praises the work of the foremost Czech nineteenth-century classic with the words: "her [Němcová's] work portrays the collective characteristics of the people, . . . she sees in the country people the hero of a new life . . . her effort is centered on the values typical of the people" (*D.* 2:584, 585).[1] It has to be added that "people's poets" or writers are not necessarily popular authors, yet they must ally themselves with the "people's revolutionary struggle." This seems somewhat natural when we read about our modern world; but it appears less obvious when the literary subject touches upon the medieval period, for which these concepts are also used.

Linguistically and conceptually related to the word *lid* is the adjective *protilidový*, meaning "directed against the people." This seems to make sense in a discussion about literature with a negative attitude toward the interests of the working class. The word, however, has still another, quite specific meaning: fiction or poetry with metaphysical or religious content might also be called *protilidové*. In this specific sense the word is top-heavy with ideology. Marxist literary history deals with *zlidovění* of cultural values, that is, about values which became the property of the people; the word was used for the period of Cyril and Methodius (ninth century) and for the fourteenth and fifteenth centuries. It is said that the hymnal *Jistebnický kancionál* [The Jistebnice hymnal] presents the Hussite movement from the vantage point of people—*s posice prolidové*. People may also use literature as a weapon against the feudal oppression; in short, people are the "hegemon literatury"—they take over the leadership in literary

1. References are to volume and page in *Dějiny* (*D.*), to page only in the one-volume *Ocherki* (*O.*).

matters. The editor of the medieval *Dalimilova kronika* [Dalimil's chronicle] claims that it supported "boj lidu" (the people's struggle).[2] The same author, in commenting on the old Czech drama, reveals that the religious aspect of medieval literature was but a cover for its social themes.[3] The first Czech translation of Erasmus' *Moriae encomium* (1511) is evaluated as a satire accessible not merely to the humanist intellectuals but to "hundreds and hundreds of simple and unsophisticated [*neučených*] people."[4]

The Marxist character of the word *lid* is also reflected in the interpretation of folklore. With the Czechs the interest in folklore goes back to the period of the Czech literary renaissance. The Czech Romantics were enthusiastically aware of the ideological potential (nationalist) of their folk poetry, and the trend has continued ever since. In the last decades of our century, the Western inquiry into folk art has stressed the irrational, abstract, and mythical aspects of it. Such an approach of course opposes the very foundation of the materialist philosophy. Although it cannot deny the irrational element of folk art entirely, Marxist theory underlines the "realistic situations" through which folk "fantasy" proceeds; folklore is a class literature par excellence and manifests the creative potential of the nation. And it has to be understood that it is always the oppressed class which represents the nation, whether in Pericles' Greece or in eighteenth-century Bohemia.

The conceptual terms *lid* (people) and *národ* (nation) stand in historical opposition to the feudal and bourgeois classes. There is, however, one word in which some of the traditional literary values of the feudal and bourgeois world survive, and this word is the expression *patriarchální* (patriarchal). It has very little in common with the biblical world of the patriarchs. The term entered the Czech Marxist vocabulary from the Russian, where it

2. Josef Hrabák, *Ze starší české literatury* (Prague, 1965), p. 84.

3. Josef Hrabák, *Staročeské drama* (Prague, 1950), p. 6.

4. Emil Pražák, *Řehoř Hrubý z Jelení* (Prague, 1964), p. 46.

fits the circumstances of the Russian prerevolutionary village incomparably better then the Czech one. *Ocherki* somewhat awkwardly used the term for the prose of J. Holeček and J. Baar and also for Jirásek's *Biedermeyer* and some parts of Hálek's poetry and prose. Even more surprising is *Ocherki*'s use of *patriarkhal'nye iliuzii* (patriarchal illusions) in the case of the impressionist poet A. Sova. The Czech *patriarchální* and the Russian *patriarkhal'nyi* are colorful words in the monochrome Marxist dictionary and cover a multitude of aspects which otherwise might lack the password into contemporary literary criticism.

The term *buržoa* (the bourgeois) is pejorative of course; the historical content of the word is defined as antihumanist, falsely philanthropic, and profaning its contemporary idea of liberty, egality, and fraternity. For the bourgeois the concept of liberty means simply freedom for ruthless exploitation.[5] Freedom belongs to "progressive" and "culturally creative" forces only.[6] A bourgeois is unable to recognize the value of art and literature. The artists Mánes and Aleš are given as examples. In reality the clientele of both artists was the Czech bourgeoisie, its institutions, and in the case of Mánes also the aristocracy. *Buržoa* is opportunist and cosmopolitan, whereas *občan* (the citizen) is revolutionary and socialist by definition. In the first quarter of our century, the bourgeois might be even a socialist-democrat who later, during the split of the Social Democratic party into Left and Right, joined the Right. The capitalist bourgeois is distinguished by his greediness, called "fetishism" of money by Czechs and Russians alike; often he would be described as antinationalist. There is only one type of praiseworthy nationalism: the revolutionary drive to realize the socialist society within one's own national group. It is for this reason that the government of the First Czechoslovak Republic is called "antinational" (*O.* 356, 358).

With the word "revolutionary," the word "progressive" (*po-*

5. Josef Špičák, *Karolina Světlá* (Prague, 1962), p. 196.

6. Bedřich Václavek, *Index*, 1938, no. 1; Květoslav Chvatík, *Bedřich Václavek a vývoj marxistické estetiky* (Prague, 1962), p. 264.

*krokový*) is perhaps the most widely used term of the official literary scholarship. *Pokrokový* literally means "allied with the interest of the people." When used about a nineteenth-century writer, it is synonymous with praise. The Czech writer Karolina Světlá (1830–99), is commended both by the *Dějiny* and *Ocherki* for her "progressive" attitude, by which is meant her criticism of the Church, her proposal for a better and more just social order, and "her nationalist idea firmly rooted in the progressive traditions of the people."[7] In a period closer to our time, the adjective "progressive" might signify the writer's ties to the party or be applied to the author who takes the position of the working class—*pozitsii rabochevo klassa* (*O.* 394). Progressive literature is the enemy of the reactionary forces. The German occupation of Czechoslovakia, for example, sought to exterminate its progressive culture. The term is also valid for the past. We read in the introduction to *Dějiny* that the nine hundred years of Czech literary history advanced progress and revolution (*D.* 1:13).

Should the word "progressive" be coupled with the word *věda* (science) or *vědecký* (scientific, scholarly), it would have a strong ideological stress. The adjective *vědecký* is often attached to the word "atheism." Why not simply atheism? Because the Marxist literary terminology wants to keep alive the idea that people enlightened by science are inevitably atheists and that atheism is (and must be) the outcome of a progressive weltanschauung. In other words, any religion (and for that matter any metaphysical point of view) contradicts science, on which our modern world rests and builds. It is for this reason that Church Slavonic might be preferably called "old Slavic." The adjective endows the word "atheism" with a persuasion-propaganda quality. The trend of thought behind it runs roughly as follows: the Russian astronauts (not the Americans) found out that the universe contains neither angels nor souls. This is a fact of *vědecký atheismus* and

7. Josef Špičák, *Karolina Světlá,* p. 135.

typical of its arguments. *Dějiny* would speak about the liquidation (*likvidace*) of the pagan world in the Czech ninth and eleventh centuries. The application of the word seems to be influenced by the Russian practice; in *Ocherki* (*O.* 152) we read, for example, about *likvidatsia boga* (liquidation of God). The word for God, of course, is never written with a capital, neither in Russian nor in Czech. More appropriately, "liquidate" may also mean the ruin of "progressive cultural tradition," whether during the Czech Counter-Reformation or during World War II.

The adjective *konkrêtní* (concrete, as opposed to abstract) is a favorite term. It appears in the idiomatic expression *konkrêtní historická situace*, which means a definite (i.e., concrete) historical situation. *Konkrêtní* always carries a positive evaluation. The medieval satires of *Hradecký Ms.* or the Hussite songs are praised for their description of concrete situations (*D.* 1:245). The word is in vogue and has acquired a nearly sacerdotal character. It appears for instance in the title *Dialektika konkrêtního*[8] [The dialectics of the concrete]. The lexical meaning may be paraphrased as dialectics of terms and ideas that are neither abstract nor general, that is, terms and ideas concerned with a certain, definite reality.

The new literary terminology does not protect the style from clichés. The generation that after World War I swept the Czech style clean of its nineteenth-century overwritten tropes would be amazed if it could witness their revival. A poet dedicates his "lyre" to the worker;[9] *plný měšec* (a bagful of money) is an attributive figure for the bourgeois. A man does not seek liberty, he "burns" for it. The Czech classic Jan Neruda was ready "to sacrifice himself in the name of liberty" (*O.* 189). To express the plight of the proletarian, both *Dějiny* and *Ocherki* use the worn out trope "calloused hands"—*mozolné ruce, mozolistye ruki* (*D.* 2:189, *O.* 124). A socialist image of a writer is the Russian word

8. Karel Kosík, *Dialektika konkretního* (Prague, 1960).

9. Jiří Beran, *O Petru Bezručovi* (Prague, 1951), p. 16.

*borets* and the Czech *bojovník* (fighter), a term applied to the modern Czech writer Marie Pujmanová and to the Czech Hussite reformer as well. Under the Russian influence of clichés like *goŕkaia ironiia* or *goriashchii patriot* (passionate irony, fervent patriot), Czech bathos thrives again.

As Marxist literary criticism approaches the present, its terminology becomes more politically involved. One of the words with newly sharpened ideological edges is *sebekritika* (self-criticism). The word goes far beyond its English equivalent. In the non-Marxist communication system, lack of self-criticism may be a relatively harmless fact. A person may think of himself as clever while others who do not share that opinion may say he lacks self-criticism. This is not necessarily a crucial situation. On the other hand, in the Marxist system the lack of *sebekritika* has ominous innuendos and may even spell danger. It could mean that one has overlooked some of one's responsibilities, which in the case of a writer may signify that he has written from his individual point of view and has neglected the collective interests. He has indulged in artistic self-complacency and lost sight of the needs of his community. Moreover, he may have considered the revolutionary process from a stationary position and failed to view it in its dynamic perspective. Lack of self-criticism may obstruct the progress of the national literature or damage the national industry. In both cases the consequences might be disastrous. The English word "self-criticism" can be used in both a positive and negative sense; the Czech *sebekritika* is used mostly in its negative aspect, as in *neprokázal dostatečnou sebekritiku* (he has shown a lack of self-criticism). Such a sentence might be read in court or in a literary magazine.

Another novum in the Czech literary dictionary is the word *autocensura*. Webster does not give its parallel. Although modern European literary history, especially that of the Slavs, abounds in references to censorship, the term is a novelty. *Autocensura* (we might say "self-censorship") seems to be a protective psychological device. It sets in automatically whenever a writer faces a blank sheet of paper; it may be imagined as a tiny computer in a writer's mind preventing him from writing anything that might incriminate him or result in trouble from the authorities. Although this concept of a brain-computer was invented to use about contemporary writers, the literary historian even applied it to J. K. Tyl, a mid-nineteenth-century writer: Tyl did not wait until his play or short story would get "killed" in the censor's office and protected his work with "autocensura."[10]

The new literary language is oriented against abstractions and formalist fetishes. In this conceptual language, personal interests do not really mean personal interests but those which may conflict with the intentions of the party. With some literary critics this terminology frequently recedes behind the usual type of literary expression until a Russian-born term, as in "unmask [*demaskovati*] the aristocracy, the authority, etc.," brings the language of the new *Wechselseitigkeit* to our awareness.

10. Mojmír Otruba and Miroslav Kačer, *Tvůrčí cesta J. K. Tyla* (Prague, 1961), p. 220.

# 8
# NEW FACADE FOR A CLASSIC

*Id est classicus adsiduusque aliquis scriptor, non proletarius.*

Aulus Gellius

A WRITER who has once been honored with the title "classic" might suffer from neglect but rarely from a considerable devaluation. To him is erected a monument *aere perennius*, on which the changes of the literary climate have but little effect. The less great, on the other hand, are subject to corrosions inflicted by the passage of time, although it may happen that these same corrosions cover the surface of the literary work with a precious patina. Marxist literary criticism, conservative and dogmatic, left the majority of its classics on their granite pedestals; it was from the group of the less prominent men that it raised some writers to a new position of esteem. Such a favorite was J. K. Tyl (1809–56), dramatist, actor, writer of fiction, and journalist. The non-Marxist literary historians did not deny him due respect, nevertheless they hesitated to place him among the great.

Tyl was an author who never cared for sophistication. All his efforts were oriented toward the entertainment and education of the Czech public. His two never-ending concerns were to secure a stage on which plays, his own and those of other playwrights, would be performed and to establish a periodical for which he would be the main writer and editor. In the poem *Zpěvcum* [To the bards, 1835] he wrote: "Pryč harfu z rukou sebemilce (Away with the harp in the hand of an egotist). In Romantic terms it was a protest against self-centered art unconcerned with the pressing cultural needs of the nation. If we were to transpose the dated language into ours, we might guess how beautifully Tyl met the demands of socialist realism. His passion for the theater and his professional experience made him a successful playwright and producer, but the meager cultural conditions of his period and the political pressure of the Bach era brought him to sheer misery. The man who in 1848 was a member of the Austrian Constituent Assembly died as a hungry trouper.

The existent literary profile of Tyl has two distinct parts. The first in chronology, the standard textbook version, as it appears in *Stručné dějiny literatury české* [A short history of Czech literature] by Arne Novák,[1] underlines Tyl's dedication to the Czech national cause, and in this it agrees with the other, the Marxist version. Novák pointed to Tyl's interest in the contemporary social problems, praised his versatile talents, and defended him against Havlíček's criticism of *Poslední Čech* [The last Čech]. Yet Novák did not hesitate to say what others perhaps only thought: that Tyl's dramas, especially those written before 1848, were mere oratory. To describe some of Tyl's prose, Novák used expressions like "cheap fictional device," "sentimental patriotism," and "larmoyant sensibility." The Marxists considered Novák's evaluation bourgeois and published new monographs and essays to correct the errors of the past.

A typical exponent of the Marxist approach toward Tyl was Zdeněk Nejedlý (1878–1962), the Czech Catiline, who never tired of forcing on his audience the names (taken as standards) of Jan Hus for the medieval period and of J. K. Tyl, B. Němcová, B. Smetana, and A. Jirásek for the nineteenth century. It was not because Nejedlý's interpretation is Marxist that it produces an unpleasant and often irritating effect; it is his stubborn

1. Novák, *Stručné dějiny literatury české* (Prague, 1946), pp. 233–36.

and repetitious conservative taste which is appalling. His criticism never leads the reader to a better understanding of the work in question but tries to impose on him the interpreter's opinions. In June 1951, Nejedlý presided over the conference commemorating the hundredth anniversary of Tyl's death. The participants cited and quoted Nejedlý repeatedly. The reason was not quite innocent: Nejedlý had an influential position and was on the best footing with both the Czech and the Russian Communist parties. The speakers acclaimed in unison Nejedlý's view of Tyl, who had often been "falsified and obscured by the capitalist middle class."[2] The politico-ideological tenor of the conference was more than obvious. It revealed the lack of "kádrové politiky v divadle" (supervisory policy in the theaters), and its conclusive message proposed Tyl as an example for the young generation, which was seen as contaminated by the evils of "egocentric individualism." The sessions closed with the following sentence: "Our examples must be the artists of the Soviet Union."[3]

The Soviets published a translation of Tyl's selected works (Josef Kaetan Tyl, *Izbrannoe* [Moscow, 1954]), and the Russian history of Czech literature emphasized the importance of Tyl's historical drama (*Jan Hus*), in which for the first time not an individual hero but the Czech nation acted as the driving force of history.[4] In close parallel with the Czech Marxist concept of Tyl, the Russian essay described his work as an antidote to the self-seeking individualist literature and as a protest against both feudalism and the newly emerging capitalist bourgeoisie, which deserted the national cause for its class interests. The article made an allowance for Tyl's limitations (for instance, his solution of the class conflict by liberal reforms), and gave him an accolade for his optimistic faith in the victory of the just cause.

2. *Živý odkaz J. K. Tyla*, Publication of the Conference of Czech Dramatists (Prague, 1952), p. 57.

3. Ibid., p. 66.

4. *Ocherki istorii cheshskoi literatury XIX–XX vekov*, p. 102.

Tyl is the author of *Fidlovačka, aneb žádný hněv a žádná rvačka* [The fair Fidlovačka, 1837], a play remembered by all Czechs for its song "Kde domov můj," which became and still is the Czech national anthem. It was not because of this Biedermeyer musical that the Marxists chose to remodel the aging appearance of Tyl's work. Their choice was guided by his historical drama, the least fit to survive on the stage, but evidently the best to live as ideology. The plays on which the Marxist criticism centered were all written around the revolutionary period of 1848. As a revolutionary cry they were already recognized at their first nights, by both the public and the police. The best known among them is *Kutnohorští havíři* [The Kutná Hora miners, 1846]. The censor of the manuscript forbade the performance on the grounds that the play portrayed insurgence and armed revolt; so the premiere of the drama did not take place until two years later, in 1848. It was produced again in 1864, 1931, and 1945; its most significant anniversary was in 1948. The festive performance enjoyed an unusual setting: it was produced in Vladislavský Sál,[5] the Gothic hall in Prague Castle where medieval tournaments were held and coronation banquets served, and where Czech barons swore fealty to their king. For the reader who has not had the opportunity to see the play or read its script, a sample of the dialogue is given below. The Czech critic Z. Š. Zdeněk described the content of the drama as the conflict between the Kutná Hora miners and their ruthless exploiters.[6] Another critic wrote, "it [*Kutnohorští havíři*] has an outstanding place in the world's historical drama because of its original portrayal of the revolutionary proletariat."[7]

*Holý* . . . we are afraid that they will put the squeeze on our wages to refill their pockets once more.

5. The reign of the Czech king Vladislav is the period in which the drama *Kutnohorští havíři* takes place.

6. Z. Š. Zdeněk, *Politický význam J. K. Tyla* (Prague, 1963), pp. 50, 51.

7. Mojmír Otruba and Miroslav Kačer, *Tvůrčí cesta J. K. Tyla* (Prague, 1961), p. 304.

*Šimon* It serves us right! Let us not pity ourselves. Why do we let them do as they please? We could have helped ourselves long ago, if we were not cowards dressed like miners.

*Opat* Is it a revolt that you propose? Do you intend to take steps which are against the law? Will you not stop before bloodshed?

*Vít* Since we are outlaws and treated as such, we do not stand under the law. And if blood should be shed, it would be the blood from the cancer of our mines. . . .

*Opat* Let's ask the Lords for negotiations, let us act in good faith and the spirit of peace. . . .

The peaceful solution, however, was blocked by the cruel and vicious administrator of the silver mines. The armed revolt of the miners was suppressed and the play ended with the words of the miner Vít, who escaped the execution: "The blood of our brothers was shed but it was not a useless sacrifice. Out of the bloodshed will grow the future seed [of the revolution]." It remains to be said that the revolutionary story is coupled with the tragic romance of two lovers separated by an infamous father, the administrator of the mines. His son, *le jeune premier*, preserves his integrity till the end, yet has to drift from the final scene while his angelic love, the daughter of the executed miner Opat, takes the veil. The president of the Czechoslovak Republic associated *Kutnohorští havíři* with socialist ideals and wrote to the director of the play: "the performance . . . was a monumental celebration of the final and victorious struggle of our miners for their social and national rights. . . ."[8]

Another of Tyl's plays connected with the year 1848, its hopes, and its temporary freedom of speech and press is *Jan Hus.* In Tyl's play this reformer, a disciple of Wycliffe, who was sentenced to death by the Council of Constance, is a Czech patriot of 1848 who recites lines about "the dawn of a new morning" and accuses the Church of opposing free intellectual developments. Tyl's king, angered by the interference of the Church in

8. Miroslav Kačer, *Josef Kajetán Tyl* (Prague, 1959), p. 252.

Czech political affairs, speaks about the separation of State and Church. The Hussite warrior Žižka warns him that the oppressed people may lose their patience and "shake the stability of thrones." The plural "thrones" was a figure of speech in 1848 as in 1948: in 1848 it meant the Austrian monarchy, in 1948 the imperialist West. During the 1848 premiere the audience applauded at places like "the foreign dynasty on the Czech throne," and those who were unable to enter the theater shouted hurrahs outside in the street. None of this escaped the Prague police, and soon further performances of the play were forbidden. The political temper of 1848 also entered *Jan Žižka* (1848), a play about the Hussite military leader. In historical reality he was opposed by the extremists of his own party, whereas in Tyl's drama he is a radical enemy not only of the king and emperor but of the feudal society. "He knew that peace was impossible with them," explained the Marxist interpreter.[9]

Nationalist ideas guided the drama *Krvavé křtiny* [The bloody christening], which became the model for the dramatic dialogue dealing with early Czech Christianity. Saint Wenceslaus and his grandmother Saint Ludmila, both martyrs, appeared in the play as detrimental to the welfare of the Czech nation because of their peace-seeking attitude toward the German emperor. The fratricide Boleslav was portrayed as a power-driven man and his mother Drahomíra as the embodiment of the Panslavic idea—she dreamed about a Slavic kingdom approximating the Great Moravian Empire. The remarks of the Marxist commentator left no ambiguity about the correct meaning of the play: "[Tyl] tore down the martyr's crown from Wenceslaus's head and . . . showed . . . that the real Wenceslaus was a weak ruler who . . . was neglecting the common Slavic interests."[10] He also called the Saint Wenceslaus tradition the tradition of "capitulation, cowardice, and treason"; it has to be understood that the Ger-

9. Zdeněk, *Politický význam J. K. Tyla*, p. 121.

10. Ibid., pp. 95, 96.

many to which Saint Wenceslaus "capitulated" was the Germany of the West.

More on the periphery of the current Czech and Russian evaluation of Tyl's work are his musicals, or "plays with songs and dances" as they were called in the essay *Klasický základ české hry se zpěvy a tanci* [The source of the Czech musical] by Eva Pensdorfová. Her essay is refreshing because she deals with facts of cultural history rarely touched upon before.[11] Pensdorfová described the Czech and Viennese Biedermeyer comedy, although she remained laconic about its heyday of Raimund and Nestroy when a visit to Leopoldstädter Theater was de rigeur even for people like Jacob Grimm or Hegel. In 1848, Tyl was in Vienna and he could not have missed some of those performances known all over Central Europe. The word "Lumpacivagabundus" (from a character's name), which survived in the Czech vernacular until our century, indicates how popular Nestroy's plays must have been among the Czechs.[12] It seems impossible that Tyl, for whom theater meant the world, would not have read or seen the play about Lumpacivagabundus or for that matter the similarly popular *Der Alpenkönig und der Menschenfeind* (1828) by Ferdinand Raimund.[13] The Czech "Alpenkönig," Krakonoš, has the role of supernatural helper in Tyl's *Tvrdohlavá žena* [The stubborn wife, 1849]. Pensdorfová preferred to enlarge upon the political references in the play, such as "Meterník" (Metternich) or "okrojírka," which was and still is the popular Czech name for the Austrian Constitution of 1849. Such political innuendos were part of the folk comedy.[14] Both Nestroy and Tyl localized

11. Arne Novák had very briefly mentioned A. Bäuerle, one author of Viennese folk comedy of which Tyl's musicals were a Czech counterpart.

12. Johann Nestroy, who had a Czech background, was also an actor; he performed in Prague in 1844. Otto Forst de Bataglia, *Johann Nestroy* (Munich, 1962), pp. 79, 114.

13. The text circulated in handwritten copies only.

14. In 1848–49, the ultraconservative Nestroy produced *Freiheit in Krahwinkel*, representing Metternich by the character Intendant Wichtig; how-

their social groups, types, and characters; both taught justice and morality and caricatured the rich and proud and greedy. The most salient similarity between the Austrian and the Czech folk comedy was their use of the intervention of the fairy-tale world in human affairs.

The originality and achievement of Tyl's musicals consisted in their use of Czech folklore, its customs, songs, and melodies. And it is because of these traditional folk elements that some of his comedies like *Strakonický dudák* [The piper from Strakonice] survived, whereas plays like *Jan Hus* or *Kutnohorští havíři* were kept alive only with the help of an ideological interpretation. The folk comedies have some of Tyl's most original and vivid characters, for example, the violinist Kalafuna, the piper Vocílka, or Švanda's lover, Dorotka, in *Strakonický dudák*. The *Märchenspiel* might still be attractive to the modern taste and not merely the Czech one. In 1962 the Viennese Burgtheater produced Raimund's *Moisarus Zauberfluch*, in which the artist Oscar Kokoschka participated.[15] And in 1954 *Strakonický dudák* was produced in Peking.[16] It would be interesting to know in which manner the Chinese understood the Czech "Zaubermärchen," whether its producers were led by Marxist interpretation —happiness should not be sought in the world of false glitter and riches or in foreign countries—or whether it was the magic of the Czech folk fantasy which appealed to their imagination.

Like his plays, Tyl's prose was written for immediate consumption, and this answers in part why it is of average quality. When Tyl chose to write about the life of the salon—which he did not often do—Havlíček's attack on him, on his empty rhetoric and sentimental clichés, seemed entirely justified. On the other hand,

---

ever, his was a theatrical satire in tune with the revolutionary spirit of the Viennese population, without Tyl's ever-present nationalist and patriotic overtones.

15. Ferdinand Raimund, *Gesammelte Werke* (Vienna, 1962), p. 29.

16. Kačer, *Josef Kajetán Tyl*, p. 225.

when he turned to a subject from the street where he lived—the shoemaker to whom he owed money, the boy apprentice, the maid from the next floor, or the grocer around the corner—he was able to create a new direction in Czech fiction. He observed the sociological pattern of Prague's life, especially of its lower middle class and proletariat, and he was keenly aware of the problems rising with the industrial revolution. It is here that Neruda's remark about Tyl, made in 1878, is worth citing: "Without Tyl modern Czech fiction is unthinkable."[17]

The Marxists do not exaggerate when they stress Tyl's effort to guide the Czech public. His editorials and articles were avidly read by people to whom the important events of the day were explained in a language which they could understand. "Jen ty mašiny roztlučme" [Let us destroy the machines, 1848] might be viewed as a trade-union article explaining to the workers the futility of opposition against the new machinery; it is not the technological progress which is the cause of unemployment and the lowering of the wages. Technology, Tyl continues, might be beneficial if handled with proper economic policy both national and individual; such policy requires a mutual understanding and cooperation between the worker and the owner of the factory. It was this proposition—to solve the conflict between the employer and his employees by reformist and liberal arbitration—which has been criticized by the Marxists: "[Tyl] did not understand the essential problem of his contemporary economic and political situation. . . ."[18] In other words, his limitations were provincial, democratic, humanist, and bourgeois.

The sample given below of Tyl's political journalism was published in *Sedlské noviny* in 1849.[19] The fictional dialogue evidently seemed less offensive than an article and had some chance of passing through the censor's office.

17. Ibid., p. vii.

18. Otruba and Kačer, *Tvůrčí cesta J. K. Tyla*, p. 250.

19. 1849, no. 10. Zdeněk, *Politický význam J. K. Tyla*, p. 87.

*Economist* (*Who has just finished reading a letter*) Here it is in black and white Mr. Capitalist. There is still God's justice in the world. Our army reaps one victory after another and before spring comes we will be able to sleep peacefully.

*Capitalist* Let us hope that you are right. I still have some doubts. The Constituent Assembly might bring us new troubles.

*Economist* The Constituent Assembly? (*He laughs and continues with confidence.*) Don't be afraid. Three hundred armed men are stronger than the Constituent Assembly; besides people put no trust in it anymore. It won't be long before—

*Industrialist* (*Happily*) I wish that what you say might come true. We shall see. Should the government ask for our cooperation, we will give it gladly, of course. Our interest is peace, nothing but peace. If only we were rid of the fear that this new freedom may blow away the roofs above our heads.

The comment on the political situation in the form of a dialogue was, so to speak, Tyl's technique. In the musical *Tvrdohlavá žena*, a character speaks about the newly decreed constitution using the colloquial term "oktrojírka"; it is noteworthy that the Austrian secretary of interior, Graf Stadion, was informed about this passage. The Czech Marxist critic Z. Š. Zdeněk called this part of Tyl's work "the people's school of politics."

There is one minor item in Tyl's bibliography which the Marxists preferred to overlook since it might seem like a spot on the smooth new facade. The pieces which were ignored, insignificant in themselves, are Tyl's homage for the birthday of the Austrian emperor and the address for his wedding.[20] In the birthday oration Čech gives thanks to the emperor for his recognition of the wrongs which have been done to the Czech nation in the past. And when the final curtain rose, the stage was supposed to show the glorified statue of Emperor Franz Joseph. The stage-poem

20. *Slavnostní hra* (1850) and *Sňatek panovníkův* (1854).

written for the imperial wedding in 1854, with an echo of the Austrian anthem at its end, had a similar form and message. Perhaps Tyl was under more severe pressures than Erben or Mácha, who had also expressed their loyalties in verse. Besides, no one who ever lived in an authoritative state or under political surveillance will blame him or them. The point is not that Tyl wrote those loyal addresses but that they were hushed up by his historians. As they invariably do with their favorite authors, Tyl's Marxist critics tended to present their literary hero as blameless as possible.

# 9
# HISTORY IS THE ISSUE

In the theory of Marxism the interpretation of history has a major significance, and indeed some of its terms were adopted by the Western world. A computer perhaps would tell us how often phrases such as "feudal society" or "capitalist society" are coupled in our media of communication. In the socialist countries such terms permeate the daily press, as well as literature and scholarship. Czech history offers to the Marxist scholar and critic rewarding material, particularly in its period of Reformation and Counter-Reformation, which are, moreover, traditional ideological themes with Czechs. The Czech mind likes to recall the Council of Constance and its main protagonist, Jan Hus, the Hussite Wars, and the battle of Bílá Hora as parts of a tragic but great past. The Czech historian František Palacký (1798–1878), often called the father of modern Czech history, formulated in terms contemporary to him this traditional trend of thought. In his monumental work *Dějiny národu českého* [History of the Czech nation, 1848–76],[1] he conceived and presented Czech history as the development of two ideas: the opposition

1. It was first published in German under the title *Geschichte von Böhmen* (1836–1867).

to Rome[2] and the struggle against the Germans. His concept carries the stamp of nineteenth-century Czech nationalism and its antagonism to the German and Catholic element of the Austrian rule. Palacký, a Protestant himself, also referred to the Czech Reformation as the highlight of the Czech past. It was he who expressed this idea in an attractive form, through which it gained wide popularity. The Czechs had also other aspects of their history in mind when they thought of the Hussite period. For them it meant a heroic time, a model of national heroism. The most popular and relatively recent exponent of this tradition is Alois Jirásek (1851–1930), with whose name the modern Czech historical novel must be identified—at least so we are told by the Russian history of Czech literature.[3] For the Russians, the Czech Reformation and Counter-Reformation are comparatively remote subjects of European intellectual history. Therefore, they accepted the Czech interpretation of this period practically at its face value, mainly through the writing of Zdeněk Nejedlý.

Zdeněk Nejedlý (1878–1962), who had been professor of musicology at Charles University before his exile in Moscow during World War II, and who became secretary of education in Communist Czechoslovakia, was known as a notorious supporter of Jirásek's fiction as well as of Smetana's music and Mánes's painting, all of them true "people's artists," according to him. His major scholarly achievement is a voluminous work on the Hussite song. His concept of the Hussite period is radical and extremist: for him, the aims of the Hussite movement were realized in the Russian Revolution with its socialization of property and culture.[4] He claims that the current idea of the medieval Church as a religious organization is entirely false: religion is a

2. In describing the development of opposition to Rome, Palacký deals with (1) the Latin rite in the first centuries of Czech Christianity, (2) the Czech Counter-Reformation, and (3) the close alliance of the Catholic Church with the Hapsburg dynasty.

3. *Ocherki istorii cheshskoi literatury XIX–XX vekov*, p. 310.

4. Zdeněk Nejedlý, *Velké osobnosti* (Prague, 1953), p. 37.

social phenomenon and has a social foundation.[5] His interpretation of the Hussite period as a social revolution was strongly opposed by his university colleague, the historian Josef Pekař (1870–1937). Pekař's monograph on the Hussite leader Žižka might be proposed as an ideological counterpart of Nejedlý's work on the Hussite song. Pekař presented Žižka differently from the nationalist Czech tradition. Against Nejedlý's presentation of the Hussite military leader as a "progressive" and "revolutionary," Pekař underlined his medieval mentality. He loathed the argument in which the name of Žižka or Jan Hus was allied with "democracy" and "progress."[6] His was a highly unpopular view within and outside the academic world. Nejedlý had as supporters not only public consensus but men like T. G. Masaryk, who subscribed to the concept of the Hussite period as the ethical summit of the Czech national past. Still, this democratic and sociological approach to the Czech Reformation would never have survived so strongly if it had not been for its anachronistic nationalist-political overtones. Without them Nejedlý's definition of Hussitism as "revolt against the feudal order" would never have taken root in the Czech mind. As it existed, it proved to be a good asset for the Communist atheistic propaganda.

All those ideas are mirrored in Jirásek's work and particularly in his trilogy, *Mezi proudy* [Great currents], *Proti všem* [Against the whole world], and *Bratrstvo* [Brotherhood]. The English reader will most probably never see those voluminous chronicles, since only a minimal part of Jirásek's historical fiction has been made available in translation. Those that are appear in *Stories and Legends of Old Prague* (London: Blackie, 1931). Obviously government-supported cultural propaganda, this translation has an introduction by Karel Čapek, whom the English knew and who was supposed to make the publication attractive. In his

5. Ibid., p. 19.

6. Josef Pekař, *Z duchovních dějin českých* (Prague, 1941), p. 79. This book was first published in 1925.

short foreword, Čapek almost apologizes for his participation in the book. He confesses that he read Jirásek's "legends" while he was still a child and calls them a "classic by democratic vote." No further guidance is proposed to this abridged translation of Czech medieval tales. Yet Jirásek cannot be dismissed as easily as that. Moreover, he was one of those writers who, like Dickens, are born raconteurs. Jirásek was seldom dull and often wrote with authority. His handicaps are those of Sir Walter Scott, to whom he was not quite aptly compared. Jirásek's heroes, clad in medieval garb, fought battles with arms borrowed from a museum, lived in castles restored in the objectionable nineteenth-century style, and imitated the medieval Czech while expressing nineteenth-century ideas and sentiments; their emotions were Victorian and their opinions liberal. But not all of Jirásek's fiction had the Middle Ages as a subject. His other no less extensive novels and short stories were placed in the Czech eighteenth century, which Jirásek knew how to evoke with much competence and charm. When the cultural documentation was not more remote than one or two generations, or when in addition he wrote about the past of his native countryside, his work was always enjoyable.

The Czech literati treated Jirásek with reserve. F. X. Šalda, though ready to give Jirásek credit for his role in the political struggle for Czechoslovak independence, refused the critic's placet to his historical fiction; he cited Taine and Croce and their negative criticism of the historical novel, and did not forget to mention Ernest Denis's unkind remark about Jirásek in particular.[7] He declared that Nejedlý's effort to establish Jirásek as one of the foremost Czech writers was doomed to failure. The efforts to which Šalda referred were Nejedlý's monographs written on the occasion of Jirásek's fiftieth and seventieth anniversaries, followed by another publication in 1926.[8] Nejedlý was fully aware

7. F. X. Šalda, *Šaldův zápisník*, 9 vols. (Prague, 1928–37) 6:321.

8. Nejedlý, *Alois Jirásek* (Prague, 1926). The two earlier publications were *Jirásek a Litomyšl* and *Jirásek a Náchodsko.*

of what he called the "prejudice against Jirásek" in the bourgeois and in his own socialist camp. He derived the "greatness" of Jirásek's historical fiction from the fact that it was written by a man from the people, about the people, and for the people, and as an example he gave the popularity of Jirásek's novels among the Czech soldiers during World War I.[9] Later he had to be more cautious in this argument of his, since the presence of the Czech Legions in Russia was and remains a delicate issue with the Russians.

According to Nejedlý, Jirásek's novel *Psohlavci* is the best description of the Czech revolution.[10] The Russian history of Czech literature uses a nearly identical expression. If one would take Nejedlý's word for it—and it seems that he does not exaggerate—*Psohlavci* in the Russian translation circulated among the Russian *muzhiki* in several thousand copies.[11] The novel has as subject matter the seventeenth-century peasant revolt in the Chodsko region. The idea for which the novel's hero Kozina fights and dies is not revolutionary freedom—as Nejedlý would like to have it—but privileges granted by old documents. In writing *Psohlavci*, Jirásek wrote as a nineteenth-century liberal for whom the "Czech historical rights" were the main argument in the Czech claims for autonomy.

Nejedlý's dogged effort to establish Jirásek as the great classic of modern Czech literature was successful to a point which probably exceeded Nejedlý's own imagination. During World War II, while in exile in Moscow, Nejedlý wrote an introduction to the 1943 Russian translation of *Staré pověsti české* (1894), titled in Russian *Starinnye skazaniia cheshskovo naroda*—the same book which in abridged form was introduced to English readers by

9. The Czech legionnaires in Russia gave to the divisions of their army names derived from Jirásek's novels, and they called each other "bratři" (brothers), as did their Hussite ancestors.

10. Nejedlý, *Alois Jirásek* (Prague, 1929), p. 105. The peasants who revolted had a dog's head as an emblem—hence their name, "Psohlavci."

11. Ibid., p. 28.

Karel Čapek. After his return to Prague, and even more after 1948, Nejedlý became a powerful man in Czechoslovak cultural affairs. Once again, and this time on an imposing scale, he was able to display his identification with Jirásek. In 1949 under his editorship, there was published the first volume of a new critical edition of Jirásek's collected works with the somewhat pompous heading *Jiráskův odkaz národu* [Jirásek's bequest to the nation]. The celebration of the hundredth anniversary of Jirásek's birth surpassed any honors given before to him or to any other Czech writer. In 1951, the Stalinist secretary of information, Václav Kopecký, represented the government during the festivities in Jirásek's birthplace Hronov. In Prague, on the stage of Národní divadlo, the scene looked almost like a session of a central committee of the Communist party. The stage was flanked by two rows of flags, with the Soviet hammer and sickle on one side and the Czechoslovak colors on the other. In the background, in the place usually reserved for the pictures of party leaders, a large portrait of Jirásek was displayed. Two rows of officials, writers, and intellectuals, with Nejedlý as their main speaker, faced the audience.

The peak of the anniversary festivities during the year was the opening of the Jirásek Museum for which, on Nejedlý's suggestion, the Renaissance summer palace Hvězda (Star), near Prague, had been selected. Its well-preserved medieval walls, built in the shape of a star, were restored and remodeled to house Jirásek's memorial. The verdant grounds, which were once a deer park, added to the royal splendor. At the opening, portraits of President Gottwald, Nejedlý, and Jirásek met the crowd at the entrance to the museum. The scene had that familiar aspect by which we recognize a Communist celebration, whether in Russia, China, or Bulgaria. The main speakers were Premier A. Zápotocký and Secretary of Information V. Kopecký. A huge marble plate on the wall inside the main entrance commemorated President Gottwald's address pledging in the name of the Czechoslovak nation allegiance to the "classical heritage" of Jirásek.

State protocol robbed Nejedlý of the first place; yet as long as Jirásek will be remembered, Nejedlý's name will not be forgotten. Jirásek's anniversary was also celebrated in Moscow. The official scene was much less impressive than in Prague; nevertheless it was accompanied by a sizable Jirásek exhibit and also by publication of a new critical eight-volume edition of his collected works.

Russian Marxist literary criticism shifted the emphasis from Jirásek's Hussite and Biedermeyer periods (the latter was never much publicized by the Marxists) to what was called the "socialist" and "revolutionary" element of his novels—that is, the peasant revolts of the sixteenth and seventeenth centuries. In 1959, R. L. Filipchikova selected for her literary analysis Jirásek's first novel, *Skaláci* [Made of stone, 1874].[12] The late critic F. X. Šalda, by no means an admirer of Jirásek, conceded to the novel of the twenty-three-year-old writer the originality of his subject (eighteenth-century Czech history) and characterized its content as "revolt of the hungry serfs."[13] The ultraconservative critic, H. Jelínek, singled out *Skaláci* and its "mass action" as a recurrent motif of Jirásek's fiction.[14]

Filipchikova, like Nejedlý, introduced Jirásek as the representative of "revoliutsionno-demokraticheskie idealy," and as the staunch defender of the socially oppressed. *Skaláci*, said Filipchikova, was written during the period which Engels described as the "second Austrian Revolution," the first of course being the revolution of 1848. According to her, the true hero of the novel is the nation—"narod stavitsia aktivnym geroiem romana." The protagonist, Jiřík, was destined to be a revolutionary; in his childhood he witnessed the cruelty of the feudal master of the region and of those who served him. Thus, revolt against

12. R. L. Filipchikova, *Roman Aloiza Iraseka "Skalaki."* Literatura Slavianskikh Narodov, vol. 4, 1959, pp. 186–214.

13. Šalda, *Šaldův zápisník*, 9 vols. (Prague, 1928–37) 2:224, 245.

14. See the introduction by Jelínek to Jirásek's *Les Têtes-de-Chien* (Paris, 1923).

social injustice was sown within him. Moreover, he was the descendant of a family of Czech Brethren conscious of their Hussite tradition, which for Filipchikova, as for Nejedlý, is but the tradition of revolt and insurgence (*krestianskie vostania* and *klassovyi protest*). With her the fact that the protagonist is a religious man is somehow lost. Jiřík's father made an unsuccessful attempt on the life of his feudal master Piccolomini and was sentenced to death. The Marxist interpreter commented: not the individual but the collective struggle for freedom is effective. We find a nearly identical sentence in the criticism of Karel Čapek's play *Bílá nemoc*.[15] Filipchikova expressed some reservations about the "idealistic" and "romantic" features of the novel's central character. Her analysis, however, is oriented mainly toward the peasant collective; she is even able to distinguish its "left wing" as opposed to its more conservative group. She also quotes in extenso the passages describing the famine and sickness which destroyed whole villages in the Náchodsko region, the historical locale of *Skaláci*. Aware of the negative criticism of the "bourgeois" critics (Šalda and Novák) concerning Jirásek, Filipchikova tries to reverse their opinion that Jirásek lacked psychological insight and that his characters were built on conventional narrative clichés. This part of her essay is the least convincing.

Filipchikova also contributed an article about Jirásek to *Chekhoslovatsko sovetskie literaturnye sviazi* [Czechoslovak-Russian literary relations];[16] it includes a five-page bibliography of Jirásek's translations into Russian and Russian criticism about him. Filipchikova follows the chronology of the translations and comments upon their historico-literary context. The first glance at the bibliographical list tells that the work preferred by the translators was the novel *Psohlavci*. Filipchikova speaks about its "acclimatization" in Russia; and indeed, already before the

15. See p. 59.

16. (Moscow, 1964), pp. 29–34.

Revolution it had seven editions. In 1920, Lunacharskii showed his copy of it to Šmeral, the Czech Communist leader. Could one imagine a parallel scene somewhere in the West? Another favorite with the Russians was *Staré pověsti české*, translated in 1899 for the first time. Gorki read it and recommended it for reading to his son Maksim. Later Russian editions reached over a million copies. These stories from medieval Czech history were also translated into Armenian, Moldavian, and other languages of the Soviet Union. In 1941, the battle scenes of *Proti všem* were translated and published as part of a campaign to provide Russian readers with Slavic literature worthy of critical times. Filipchikova also mentioned in the bibliography V. N. Zalezhskii's foreword to *Psohlavci* (1925), which informed the Russian reader about the Czech peasant revolt of 1693, the historical reality behind the novel.

This historical approach is paralleled in the afterword to a recent translation (1961) of Jirásek's *Filosofská historie*, offered to the English reader under the mediating Latin title *Gaudeamus igitur*. Another cultural propaganda translation, it has been made available through the publishing house Artia. The novel, a story about student life at the time of the Czech Biedermeyer, which some historians call "Vormärz" (*doba předbřeznová*), conveys the cultural atmosphere of Central Europe between the Napoleonic Wars and the year 1848. The locale of this short novel is the town Litomyšl, where Jirásek started his college teaching career. At that time he was a young man and had just finished his own studies. The provincial town supplied the budding writer with many documents on the past. He had only to listen to the yarns of his landlady or look up at the gables of the house opposite his windows to meet history. This idyllic town was also witness to the year 1848, but for its people and institutions that was a mere echo of a distant earthquake. Only one student in *Gaudeamus igitur*, the schlemiel of the group, died on the Prague barricades of 1848. In Jirásek's story, that year had the appeal of a colored lithograph which has a dated charm and shows none of the disturbing sides of the history. In this work, Jirásek might be compared to Trollope. Perhaps Jirásek's wit is not as sharp as that of the English novelist, nor is he able to dissociate himself from his protagonists as Trollope can; yet in places the atmosphere of traditional life seems to breathe a similar intimacy and charm. The figure of the provincial magistrate Rolínek, for example, equals Trollope's best.

The editors of *Gaudeamus igitur* had of course other aims than to acquaint the English reader with this side of Jirásek's fiction. The afterword to the book was written by the foremost contemporary Czech historian and not by a literary critic, as one would expect. The essay has the title "A Poetic Idyll and Historical Reality" and is signed by Josef Polišenský. One reads little about the fiction; on the other hand, one learns a great deal about the social history of the region where the poetic idyll takes place. We read about the Thirty Years War, the peasant uprisings of the seventeenth and eighteenth centuries (1680, 1775), and the economic plight which was their background—in short, more about the backdrop of the novels *Skaláci* and *Psohlavci*, and less about *Gaudeamus igitur*. Once more the issue is Marxist history. There is a reverse side to this Marxist portrait of the nation's classic. It is known that after World War I Jirásek voiced a protest against the Bolsheviks. This document, unlike Čapek's "Why I am not a Communist," which is now openly discussed, must be buried somewhere among the *acti prohibiti*, perhaps even in a sealed vault of Jirásek's own museum.

# 10

# DEVĚTSIL

IT DOES not often happen that an avant-garde movement takes for its emblem a botanical name and in addition is able to bequeath it to literary history, as did the group who called themselves Devětsil (*Petasites hybridus*). The name also has a semantic turn: *devět* (nine), *sil* (forces). Nine Muses? Perhaps, but the poets, writers, and artists who formed the group were little inclined to classicist imagery; the reference most probably was dadaist.

As much as the two countries differed in later years, in the post–World War I period the new Czechoslovakia and new Soviet Russia had in common a sense of beginning an era. The self-confidence of the Czechoslovak Republic encouraged ambitious minds. Embassies opened in Prague and new possibilities arose for those who sought international intellectual exchange. The literary avant-garde was confident that it could practice an independent art and literature. In terms of history it was to be a short-lived illusion. After a decade it was clear that the Czechoslovak writer was once more confronted with politico-ideological issues and responsibilities. However, in those early twenties, a period of prosperity seemed ahead. Karel Čapek and Jaroslav Hašek were yet to write their masterpieces and Vítězslav Nezval to earn his poet's laurels. It was in the Devětsil group, from which Nezval emerged as one of the dominant figures in Czech literature, that the future ideological drama and its course were seeded.

When the Communist party established its headquarters in Czechoslovakia, it found a favorable reception among the Czech and Slovak intellectuals. From the beginning it knew how to attract writers and poets.[1] In this respect its policy might be called Machiavellian in the best sense of the word. Cultural relations between Czechoslovakia and the USSR were harmonious. The Society for Culture and Economic Exchange with the New Russia (*Společnost pro kulturní a hospodářské styky s novým Ruskem*), which was founded in 1925, had the support of the intellectual Left and was tolerated by the government. Perhaps the Czech public was not quite familiar with the poetry of Maiakovskii, but it crowded performances of *Bronenosec Potemkin* [The battleship Potemkin, 1926], directed by Eisenstein, and all guest performances by the Russian theater. Meierkhold was the model for the young Czech dramatist. The Czech and Slovak writers and artists were guests in the Villa Tereza, the site of the Soviet diplomatic representation and later its embassy; Maiakovskii lived there during his visit in 1929. As if symbolically, it was located in Žižkov, the section of Prague associated with the city's proletariat. The majority of embassies were situated in the palaces of the old city, but the Soviets made a different choice, perhaps perforce.

One of the guests at the villa, the Slovak Laco Novomeský, left us a poetic memoir (*Vila Tereza*, 1963) dedicated to the Soviet envoy A. A. Ovseienko and to other comrades and friends of those days. The memoir's central personae, the host and the

1. See *Ocherki istorii cheshskoi literatury XIX–XX vekov*, p. 384.

poet himself, were later politically persecuted, and out of the "friends and comrades" only the poet survived:

*Čas všetko vyriešil*
*alebo aspoň mnoho.*

He reviews the avant-garde of that time: "chlapci z Mánesa . . . Disk, Pásmo, Dav a Avantgarda, / Dědrasbor s proletkultom, džes, Tam-tam a Dada. . . / A boli polemiky, kriky, hovory a spory. . . ." There were unending discussions in cafés. Sometimes coffee and rolls were charged to the headwaiter; at Villa Tereza the refreshments were free:

*A môžeš do bufetu*
*po tanierek a naň. . . .*

*Vila Tereza* refers to Devětsil, to the collection of poetry by Nezval and Biebel, to Teige and Seifert, and to the secretariat of the Central Committee of the Czechoslovak Communist party. It quotes Vančura: "Nová je hvězda komunizmu . . . a mimo ní není modernosti . . ." (New, new is the Red Star . . . and modern art cannot live elsewhere). The Soviet orientation did not prevent Czech intellectuals from promoting the drama of Brecht or the art of Picasso, Léger, Chagall, Brancusi, and Grosz. Chaplin's *The Kid* (1920) was considered to be a great aesthetic experience.

Between the "gay twenties" dominated by Teige as the leader of Devětsil and the amnesty of the living and dead writers of the sixties, extends a memorable chapter of the history of Czechoslovak literary Marxism. The Czechoslovak Communist party was founded in 1922, and a few years later the leftist intellectuals were faced with their first ideological test. The fifth Congress of the Czechoslovak Communist party imposed new directives on its members. Several writers—Neumann, Olbracht, Majerová, Vančura, and Seifert among them—left the party, since they felt that the new cultural policy threatened their artistic freedom. The Devětsil group—Clementis, Fučík, Nezval, Novomeský, Teige, and Václavek—on the other hand, underlined the dependence of modern culture on the workers' movement.[2] The future was to reveal that this very loyal avant-garde was preg-

2. Květoslav Chvatík, *Bedřich Václavek a vývoj marxistické estetiky* (Prague, 1962), p. 111.

nant not merely with heroes (Fučík and Václavek) but also with "traitors" (Clementis, who was the postwar minister of foreign affairs, Novomeský, and Teige). At that time one thing was evident and beyond doubt: the party asked for obedience and discipline in matters of art and literature. Still, the sharp dangerous edges and the essence of the problem remained latent. Those were to appear in the thirties, when Václavek exposed the error of people who refused to surrender to the policy of the party. Václavek further clarified the difference between democratic-bourgeois and socialist-democratic freedom, the latter being the privilege of the progressive and creative social and cultural forces; any other kind of freedom was simply anarchy in the realm of ideas and art.[3] In 1938, when this was written, the threat to Czechoslovak national freedom overshadowed the ideological tenets of literary Marxism. Those, however, who read *Index*—(its cover slogan read: *SSSR udarnaia brigada proletariata vsevo mira*—USSR, the shock-brigade of proletarians from all over the world) in which Václavek's article "Literatura a svoboda" [Literature and freedom] was published, and particularly those who were able to read it understandingly, could have foreseen the purge which might follow should the power behind Václavek's theory ever enforce it.

Bedřich Václavek (1897–1943) started as a student of Czech literature under the ultraconservative professors Jaroslav Vlček and Jan Jakubec. As one may guess from the pages of his diary, he must have been an ambitious young man. He joined Devětsil in 1920, and with Teige, Nezval, and Seifert sincerely believed in revolution, in Lenin, in Soviet Russia, and in the Third International. In between the lines of his diary, one may sense that he wished to be not merely a scholar and critic but perhaps also a poet. But he had neither Nezval's nor Seifert's vivid response to modern poetry, nor Teige's gift for criticism. In spite of his later, permanent place in Czech literary history, he was just "der

3. Ibid., pp. 264, 265; *Index* 10, 1938, no. 5.

tüchtigste junge Mensch,"[4] as he was described by his professor, the Germanist and literary critic Otokar Fischer. His "Tüchtigkeit" was precisely what the party needed. Like Karel Čapek, Václavek studied in Berlin, where he became familiar with German revolutionary literature and its concept of the political mission of the artist.[5] The direct influence of writers like Lu Märten and W. Hausenstein can be easily spotted in his *Poesie v rozpacích* [Poetry is embarrassed, 1930], considered to be the first Marxist formulation of aesthetic problems in Czechoslovakia.

In 1928 Václavek published *Od umění k tvorbě* [Art and creativity], an answer to Teige's *Stavba a báseň* [Structure and poetry], which had appeared the year before. The future dissension was already, if only potentially, present: Václavek proposed as the cornerstone of aesthetics Marxist sociology with its stress on the content of the literary work, whereas for Teige the formal aspect of art remained important. Teige had the advantage of close cooperation with contemporary poets. Nezval by his *Pantomima* [Pantomime, 1924] and Seifert by his *Na vlnách T.S.F.* [Over the wireless, 1925] backed Teige's theory; Václavek had the powerful Communist International behind him. He took part in the Second International Congress of the proletarian and revolutionary writers at Kharkov in 1930, and returned a changed man. What before was a mixture of groping scholarship and enthusiasm for modern directions became strict ideological discipline. In Germany fascism was rising and in Russia socialist realism was taking definite shape.[6] The first Congress of Soviet Writers served to disseminate the official blueprint of socialist realism both at home and abroad. At that time Gottwald, the future Communist president of Czechoslovakia, was at the head of the Czechoslovak Communist party, and working under him was a phalanx of militant intellectuals whose names

4. Bedřich Václavek, *Deník, 1921–1922* (Olomouc, 1962), p. 21.

5. He edited *K marxistické estetice* (Prague, 1934), a collection of essays by German leftist writers.

6. *Literaturnaia gazeta*, 29 May 1932.

were to be better known after World War II: Ladislav Štoll, Kurt Konrád, Eduard Urx, Jiří Taufer, F. C. Weiskopf, and Julius Fučík. *Tvorba*, the party's literary weekly, was the bulwark of Marxist cultural propaganda.

The first Congress of Soviet Writers (1934) was a significant experience for its Czechoslovak participants. Nezval did not allow politics to interfere with his surrealist dream about Moscow or with his delightful erotic sensations in Moscow's crowded trolley cars. His friends Teige and Hoffmeister, less surrealist minded, saw the handwriting on the walls of the congress and in the comments of the press. They tried to salvage modern art as they understood it, and hoped or believed that this could be done. They argued that socialist realism must not be identified with the descriptive and psychological realism of the preceding century, that is, with conservative art and literature. Václavek, the diligent (*tüchtig*) student, on the other hand, listened to the speeches at the Congress with a receptive mind. It was not opportunism which made him adopt without reservations the Soviet socialist realism; in this he was guided by his own inclination. His first literary interest was in the field of the popular folk song and not in the poetry of an Apollinaire or a Maiakovskii. While for Hoffmeister and many others the Russian turn from futurism, cubism, and modern architecture was personally painful, for Václavek it was but a necessary and logical step. He criticized the Czech avant-garde for its neglect of the "heritage of the past," and this again not so much because it was the Communist order of the day, but because such was essentially his own taste. His former association with Devětsil and its ultramodernism was not a camouflage but merely the step of a diligent young man anxious to be part of the leading group of his time.

At the 1934 congress—he may have seen there Aragon, Hemingway, and Brecht—Václavek understood that things had changed and that this change had historical importance. He put his bet on its victory. Although he must have been aware that Teige's Marxism was as genuine as his own and that both

Teige and Nezval sincerely believed in the coexistence of surrealism and Communism, nevertheless he objected that their effort to bridge the cultural trends of East and West was often made "at the expense of the East."[7] Surrealism was not as yet branded by the party as a deviation (in 1933 in *Tvorba,* Teige pronounced surrealism "revolutionary"); nevertheless it was already then regarded as a weakening influence on the socialist idea. While Nezval was foolish enough (history showed that he was the only one who could afford such extravagance) to proclaim publicly that poetry was independent of democracy and dictatorship,[8] Václavek "knew" that this was all wrong and pleaded for a change of "individualist culture into a collective, one."[9] Still, the cohesiveness of the Czechoslovak intellectual Left, its outward unity, the support which it got from the party, all these permitted Václavek to work side by side with Nezval whom he considered to be a great poet, and to a certain point with Teige, even if the distance between them was critically widening.

In the meantime, Ladislav Štoll, who ten years or so later was to come out as the official spokesman for the Stalinist socialist realism, joined the surrealist and socialist dialogue. The occasion was the collective publication *Surrealismus v diskusi* [Discussion of surrealism, 1934], in which Teige published a passionate defense of surrealism, in reality an apology for modern art. He claimed that there was nothing in surrealism which could oppose Marxism—an argument used some ten years later by the Czech intellectuals in defense of modern art and literature on behalf of the Russian poets Akhmatova and Pasternak. Teige had already written with a certain nostalgia and regret for the time when "the patron of Czech poetism was Guillaume Apolli-

7. Chvatík, *Bedřich Václavek a vývoj marxistické estetiky,* app., p. 230.

8. V. Nezval, "*Přednáška o avantgardní literatuře,*" in Chvatík, *Bedřich Václavek,* p. 269. The essay was orginally given as a lecture in 1930.

9. Bedřich Václavek, "Poesie v rozpacích," in Chvatík, *Bedřich Václavek,* p. 276. The essay was written in 1930.

naire, whose *Alcools* and *Calligrames* decided the fate of Czech poetry."[10] Teige's opponent Štoll conceded to him that the surrealists supported the proletarian revolution but objected to their subjective vision of the world. Others joined the discussion and spoke for or against the compatibility of surrealism with dialectical materialism and proletarian revolution. The conclusive pages were signed by Teige and Štoll with the proviso that the relationship between surrealism and socialist realism remain open for further discussion. Teige did not know and could not know that he was signing his doom. He continued his hopeless opposition and was unable to resign himself to disown the days when Maiakovskii was the guest of Devětsil[11] and when Lenin and Lunacharskii supported futurism.

The Communist literary offensive was turning radical. Kurt Konrád (1908–41), a typical *popushchik*, accused surrealism of escapism, and instead of French surrealist poetry and prose he promoted such Russian novels as *Den' vtoroi* [The second day] by I. G. Ehrenburg, *Podniataia tselina* [Virgin soil upturned] by M. A. Sholokhov, and *Vremia vpered* [Time, forward!] by V. P Kataev.[12] Václavek in 1937 wrote out a few suggestions for tactics: "Expose the ideological deviations of the so-called avant-garde. [Whom else but Teige could he have had in mind?] Preserve a *cautious* [italics mine] cooperation with the center. Attack . . . the Catholics as far as they have fascist affiliations . . . be aggressive toward ruralists."[13] Nezval showed flexibility. His domain was poetry and not ideology. As volubly as he reported to the party the formation of the Czechoslovak surrealist group in 1934, just as dutifully did he submit to its disbandment in 1938. One of Nezval's often cited poems has the title *Odevzdal jsem svůj lístek ve znamení revoluce* [I voted for revolution]. Teige

10. *Surrealismus v diskusi* (Prague, 1934), p. 15.

11. Karel Teige, *Vladimír Majakovskij* (Prague, 1936).

12. Kurt Konrád, *Ztvárněte skutečnost* (Prague, 1963).

13. Chvatík, *Bedřich Václavek a vývoj marxistické estetiky*, p. 243.

and Václavek also voted for revolution and pledged their party membership and, though for different reasons, lost. Václavek was executed by the Nazis, and Teige was one of those for whom the amnesty after Stalin's death came too late. Nezval was the winner. His talent, even if often squandered and misused, was above the vicissitudes of surrealism and socialist realism. Poets enjoy an advantage which ideologists miss: their verses—the good ones—outlive the theories in which they shared.

# 11
# A POET IS A POET IS A POET

SOME may not appreciate Nezval's poetry, yet they will have to recognize his dominant role among Czechoslovak poets in the years between the two world wars. His great honors came mainly after World War II, although the formation of his talent and his most important achievements took place before that time.

Nezval introduced himself in person to the Russian audience at the memorable Congress of Soviet Writers in 1934; at that time his obsession with surrealism—it cannot be called otherwise—certainly could not have made a favorable impression on his hosts. More recently in Czechoslovakia, Nezval's surrealism has been explained as an escape from the pressures of the bourgeois society into dream and its subconscious. During the thirties, Nezval maintained that surrealism was revolutionary and that Breton and his associates were progressive artists.[1] Already in 1924 Nezval had written a poem on Lenin's death, and in 1929 when some of the Czech Communist writers rebelled against the new look of the Czechoslovak Communist party, Nezval was one of the faithful who proclaimed the solidarity of culture with the proletariat. In 1949 he published the poem *Stalin* with the fol-

1. Antonín Jelínek, *Vítězslav Nezval* (Prague, 1961), pp. 60, 79.

lowing dedication: "Báseň k sedmdesátým narozeninám Generalissima Josipa Vissarionoviče Stalina" (Poem for the seventieth birthday of Generalissimo Iosip Vissarionovich Stalin). The word "generalissimo" was used by Nezval with linguistic relish, though he must have been familiar with its dictatorial connotations. The poem followed the biographical and historical facts of Stalin's life and did not hesitate to flatter.

*Car, císař, král a diplomacie*
*se smečkou hrabat, Rotschildů a grófů*
*a sociální demokracie*
*uvrhli celé lidstvo v katastrofu.*

("Czar, emperor, king and diplomats, with a pack of aristocrats, Rothschilds, and social democrats, brought catastrophe upon all mankind.") With one exception (*hrabat* and *grófů* were translated by "aristocrats"), there is little difference between the paraphrase and the original. If it were not for the rhyme, it would be very easy to translate this poem, which enumerates the names of Kornilov, Zinovev, Kamenev, Bucharin, Trotsky, Kerenskii, Denikin, Wrangel, Chamberlain, Churchill, Goering, and Hitler. All these men aimed at the annihilation of the "land of Stalin," either in war or in peace. Stalin, however, outwitted them; he is a born leader (*vůdce, tamada*) loved and venerated by his people; he is the commander-in-chief of the Red Army which liberated the poet's country.

The poem *Stalin* is not an isolated instance which established Nezval's reputation in Soviet Russia. His *Pochod rudé internacionály* [March of the Red International], a Czech *Levyi march* [Left march], is another obvious reason for his Russian renown.

*Kráčí*
*kráčí*
*kráčí*
*proletariát*

("Marching, marching, marching, proletariat") echoes the line "Dvizhutsia, dvizhutsia, dvizhutsia, dvizhutsia" of Bednyi's

*Glavnaia ulitsa*, which was translated into Czech in 1922. The form comes from Nezval's futurist period and depends largely on such poems by Maiakovskii as *Vladimir Il'ich Lenin:*

*Vremia—*
*nachinaiu*
*pro Lenina rasskaz . . .*

("The time has come / I begin / the story of Lenin") or *Bruklinskii most* [Brooklyn bridge]; all three were written in the period 1925–30.[2] Should the lines of Nezval's march appear conventionally printed, as in the example below, the poem would become a trivial folk ballad:

*Proletariat už kráčí hrozná vzpoura*
*Evropa se bortí, Evropa se bourá.*

("The proletariat is marching, mutiny ahead / old Europe crumbles, torn from its bed.") However, N. S. Nikolaeva, the author of a very good essay[3] on translations from Nezval's poetry into Russian, did feel in the rhythm of Nezval's *International* the resounding steps of revolution.

The editors and translators of the Russian collection of Nezval's poetry selected *Oda na návrat Karla Hynka Máchy* [Ode for the return of Karel Hynek Mácha, 1939] for the volume. In tune with Marxist patriotism, the *Ode* is a dirge on the Czechoslovak national disaster of 1938–39; Nikolaeva gave one of its stanzas as an example of translation and interpretation.

*Buď zdráva vlasti má tvé otevřené hroby*
*Nám vyhrožují zlatým křížem svým*
*Když jsi se dožila tak neúprosné doby*
*Buď aspoň vlasti milosrdná k nim.*[4]

2. Jan Jíša, *Česká poesie dvacátých let a básníci sovětského Ruska* (Prague, 1956), p. 189.

3. *Chekhoslovatsko sovetskie literaturnye sviazi* (Moscow, 1964), pp. 182–216.

4. Salute, my country, your open graves / threaten us with their golden cross / since you grew up to witness these merciless times / be kind to them, at least.

Here is the Russian word-by-word translation given by Nikolaeva:

> *Bud' blagoslavenna rodina moia, tvoi otkrytye mogily*
> *Nam ugrozhaiut zolotym krestom svoim.*
> *Esli uzh ty dozhdalas' stol' besposhchadnykh vremen*
> *Bud', rodina, khotia by milosrdna k nim*

and here the translation by M. Iarmush:

> *Blagoslovenna rodina! Grobnitsy*
> *Otkrytye krestami nam groziat.*
> *Kogda vragi narushili granitsu*
> *Tebe zhestokoserdnoi byt' nel'zia.*

The critical point of translation is line 3 of the stanza. The word-by-word translation is close to the original, which says: "Since you [my country] lived to see the merciless times." The translator interpreted freely—"at the time [when] the enemy attacked the border." Is such translating permissible? Nikolaeva answered yes. She called this license "historical commentary" and suggested that at the time when the poem was written, it would have been impossible for its author to express himself as directly as did his translator-interpreter—an unusual argument for the freedom of translation.

The poem was published in *Izbrannoe* [Collected works, 1960], a publication which the Czech critic M. Blahynka called "monumental."[5] It has 704 pages with 755 poems. In comparison with the translations into other languages—French and German—it is monumental indeed. A host of translators worked on *Izbrannoe*, including such distinguished poets as Pasternak and Akhmatova. Perhaps it is superfluous to add that neither of them chose for translation poems such as *Stalin.* Pasternak translated the long poem *Signál času* [Time signal, 1931] which repeats some motifs of Nezval's *Edison* (1928). The critical late twenties and early thirties exercised their pressure both on the Czech and the

5. *Československo-sovětské literární vztahy v období meziválečném* (Prague, 1965), p. 145.

Russian poet, and in *Signál času* Pasternak could read thoughts and emotions in which he was able to share. When Pasternak talked to Nezval at the Café Metropole, he was in his forties and his *Zhivago* was not yet written; when he was translating *Signál času* (*Signal vremeni* in Russian), he was seventy years old.

Compare Nezval's original stanza:

*Byli stavitelé sfing a pyramid*
*byli kupčíci jež vyhnal z chrámu lid*
*byli amfiteatry a katakomby*
*kněží nevolníci dusičnaté bomby*[6]

and Pasternak's translation:

*Byli sfinksy, antichnye drama,*
*Torgashchei izgoniali iz khrama,*
*Byli tsirki, veka katakomb*
(*nyne vremia udushlivykh bomb*).

Pasternak followed the original *a a b b* rhyme and condensed *Byli stavitelé sfing* into *sfinksy*, which for its part absorbed the next image, *pyramid;* a new image was added in exchange, *antichnye drama.* In the second line, Pasternak omitted the anaphoric *byli*, the clause, and its *lid* (people, crowd, mob) in favor of a more direct and less demagogic formulation. Even more significant is the suppression of *knčží nevolníci* (priests, serfs), which was replaced by *nyne vremia.* Thus Nezval's bomb of the First World War became the destructive power of "our times." Nikolaeva heard in Pasternak's interpretation a contemporary ring. One may speculate about how the poets used the adjective *dusičnatý* and *udushlivý;* the root of both adjectives is *duch.* The Czech adjective is derived from the imperfective verb *dusiti* (choke) and is also used in chemistry; the Russian adjective derives from the perfective verb *udushit'* (choke). A bomb can be not only an instrument of extermination and death by suffocation

6. There were builders of sphinxes and pyramids / there were merchants chased from the temple / there were amphitheaters and catacombs, / priests, slaves, nitric bombs.

but also a catastrophic weapon which no word of poetry could survive. Perhaps the translation suggests it more explicitly than the Czech original. Pasternak must have worked on the translation with dedication; he made two variants of the thirty-eight lines beginning with the verse "Z pražské hvězdárny se hlásil k slovu čas . . ." (Time was calling from the Prague Observatory).

Nezval's most popular poem in Russian is *Píseň míru* [Song of peace]. Written during the Korean War and translated by S. Kirsanov, *Píseň míru* is Picasso's dove in verse. Its general acclaim in the Communist world may be easily understood. Versified in a clearly set pattern, with its constant refrain at *c—zpívám píseň míru* (singing the song of peace), it aligns personalities whom one might (or might not) associate with peace: Beethoven, Mme Joliot-Curie, Klement Gottwald, and Stalin. Nezval used worn out tropes like *hudba Smetanovy řeky*—the river (*řeka*) is "Vltava," the title of the first part of Smetana's symphonic poem *Má vlast* [My country]; this metonymy was used before and after him, by Majerová, Pujmanová, Neumann, and many others in poetry, prose, and journalism.

Nevertheless, *Píseň míru* has stanzas written by a poet:

*Pro modré vlny valčíků*
*lidové písničkářky Vídně*
*až usměje se na nás vlídně*
*spod třešňového deštníku.*

This is by no means great poetry, but poetry it is. Vienna is personified by a folk singer who smiles on us invitingly from beneath her cherry umbrella. If Nezval had not been the poet he was, instead of *spod třešňového deštníku*, he might have written *spod třešňového klobouku* (beneath a cherry-trimmed hat). Of course his choice was also determined by rhyme. Moreover, he inverted "blue waves of Danube" into the unexpected "blue waves of waltzes." The stanza is typical of Nezval's nonchalance and reminds us, particularly the cherry umbrella, of his surrealist period. The dove-peace-song ends with a challenge to Wall

Street. Because of its international and "socialist-realist" content, it presented no major difficulties to the translator. It was not a new, opportunist direction of Nezval's poetry. Even during the thirties, while he was deeply immersed in surrealism, his poetry had "sovremennoe zvuchanie." The collection with the surrealist title *Skleněný havelok* [The glass havelock], contained *Budoucí válka* [The future war], later included in the Russian collection:

*Z Hradčan budou rozvaliny*
*A to čeká všechna města*
*Paříž Londýn Řím Cařihrad i tebe krásná Venezie*
*Až bude vše srovnáno se zemí*
*Pro deset miliardářů nastane doba šílené konjunktury.*

("Prague Castle will be in ruins and its fate will be that of Paris, London, Rome, Constantinople, and yours, beautiful Venice, too. When everything will be leveled to the ground, the time of mad prosperity will come for ten billionaires.")

It is understandable that Russians were primarily interested in Nezval's ideological oratory; yet they did not neglect his lyric verse. From the collection *Lirika* which followed *Izbrannoe*, Nikolaeva selected for her analysis Nezval's sonnet *Odpočinutí* [Rest],[7] translated by A. Akhmatova and D. Bobyshev. In the contest between the two interpreters, it is Akhmatova who wins. Like Pasternak, she brought to her interpretation her own poetic medium. Like Pasternak, she made changes. She translated the line "V tom čirém vzduchu pil jsem svěží vůně" into Russian as "Sredi rosistykh trav vpival ia chistyi vozdukh";[8] Akhmatova transposed Nezval's image and gave it new visual potential with "rosistykh trav." In the last line of the sonnet, on the other hand, she remained close to the original—much closer than Bobyshev—preserving its alluring qualities and even adding a new shade.

7. From the collection *Hra v kostky*, 1927–28.

8. In the clear air I drank the fragrant freshness [Czech]. On the dew besprinkled grass I drank the pure air [Russian].

*Izbrannoe* also included some of Nezval's lyric verse such as *Praha o velikonocích* [Prague at Easter]. The subject is perennial in Czech poetry but Nezval succeeded in making it sound new. The language swings freely from a simple line, "jsi hezká" (you [Prague] are pretty), to complicated tropes:

*Křehotino*
*z kamenných kosatců*
*jako psí víno*
*rostou vousy tvých paláců. . . .*

("Fragile irises hewn out of stone, your old palaces grow beards of climbing vines.") The stanza is a problem for the translator, not merely as translation but also as poetic transposition. One has to know the reality to appreciate the subtlety of Nezval's images; moreover, one has to know the variations on this theme in the past in order to be aware of the charm and novelty of Nezval's metaphors.

N. S. Nikolaeva compared two translations of Nezval's lyric *Září* (September), which in the original reads:

*Podzim už platí listím*
*svou útratu.*
*Je konec láskám, konec nenávistím,*
*a není návratu.*[9]

Nikolaeva noticed that the two first lines have the key position in the whole poem and felt that they fared much better in the translation by D. Samoilov than by I. Ivanov. Samoilov preserved the original image:

*Podzim už platí listím . . .*

*Uzh osen' listiami platit . . .*

while Ivanov changed it:

*roniaet osen' zoloto listy. . . .*[10]

9. Fall pays its debts / with leaves. / Ends loves, ends hatreds, / no turning back [Nezval].

10. Fall sheds the golden leaves . . . [Ivanov].

Nikolaeva pointed to Ivanov's use of the classical five-foot iambic line, worn by a century of practice, and as example gave Pushkin's line:

*Roniaet les bagrianyi svoi ubor. . . .*[11]

She added that Ivanov's translation echoed the classical Russian intonation rather than that of Nezval.

Nezval himself fought the poetic cliché; his work stands as a milestone between the poetic idiom as it existed before World War I and after it. A great part of his importance in the development of modern Czech poetry lies in his revolt against the traditional forms and against the traditional poetic language. In an essay on modern poetry he wrote:

> "Girls beautiful as roses [*Dívky krásné jako růže*]." No! this is all wrong. How much better to stand above a bed of roses and say: "Roses and beautiful women." You will scent the perfume which you never noticed before. And roses will be roses more than ever.[12]

It could be that Nezval never read Gertrude Stein's famous sentence; yet he might have spotted it in a Czech magazine, or his well-read and well-informed friend Teige might have told him that "a rose is a rose is a rose." Nezval did not need to be told; he knew it by instinct because, in spite of his prolixity, he was a poet who was a poet who was a poet. In 1950, at the occasion of one of the writers' meetings at Dobříš, Nezval evaluated his own poetry: ". . . I accomplished a certain limpidity of verse, a simplicity of rhythm, a directness of tone."[13] Much more may be said about his poetry, but nothing so true.

11. Woods shed their copper coat. . . [Pushkin].

12. Vítězslav Nezval, *Moderní poesie* (Prague, 1958), p. 48.

13. Jelínek, *Vítězslav Nezval*, p. 93.

# 12
# FOR THE GOOD OF THE CAUSE

CZECH and Slovak literatures were not idle bystanders when the Russian army entered the capital of Czechoslovakia in May 1945. The soldiers of General T. S. Koniev were greeted with many poems by those who had already "found their way into the Czechoslovak Communist party, accepted its program, and were speaking for the Communist cause."[1] In 1948 Klement Gottwald was the president of the Czechoslovak Socialist Republic, and a sizeable number of literati whom he knew personally stepped into the limelight. Vítěslav Nezval, the never seriously challenged poet laureate, added new distinctions to his previous honors. The old guard, men such as I. Olbracht, who in the twenties spoke with Lenin, or S. K. Neumann, the militant bearer of the red flag, all received rewards according to their loyalties of the past. The political tension of the period 1945–48 must have been promising to many and frightening to some others. Socialist realism seemed a "permanent" solution. The party dispensed directives and everyone listened. Vítězslav Nezval with his usual gusto wrote poems on Stalin and his "eternal youth," and on

1. Ladislav Štoll, *Z bojů na levé frontě* (Prague, 1964), p. 7.

Gottwald's pipe. He insisted on being treated like a favorite of the Muses and protected by them. He now enjoyed a flight above the Caucasus as once he did a stroll along the boulevards of Paris. The Czech and Slovak writers were treated like the elite of the nation.

All these real and illusory splendors did not quite bring the looked-for results. Strangely enough, many of the well-known writers did not achieve what was expected of them. Not that they met with obstacles from the outside; rather, it was their own talent which seemed to have betrayed them. An eloquent case was Jan Drda (born in 1915), who after the immediate response to his *Němá barikáda* (The silent barricade, 1945) with subjects from Prague's May uprising and the German occupation, and after his reportage from the south of Soviet Russia, *Krásná Tortiza* [The beautiful Tortiza, 1952], receded into a kind of official obscurity. Before he could consider himself the heir of Čapek's popularity—for some time he worked on the same newspaper that Čapek had—his *Městečko na dlani* [The little town, 1940], his first great success, and *Němá barikáda* were published in new editions and translated into Russian. His books continued to bring to the state publishing business over one and a half million crowns of net profit;[2] nevertheless his grip was gone.

Other authors of the late forties and early fifties owed their interest to recent history—German concentration camps, the German occupation, and the resistance movement; the issues attached to their works helped to cover the fact that literary affairs, though politically ebullient, were artistically stagnant. Nor could it be concealed that socialist-realist subjects, such as shock-work and the five-year-plan, were of interest only as long as their politico-cultural frame of reference continued. In spite of the outer show, it became evident that Czechoslovak literature could not live by party tenets only. Stalin's death and the condemnation of dogmatism and the cult of the personality found

2. *Plamen*, 1967 no. 8, p. 9.

Czechoslovak literature ready for a change. Almost all the prominent prewar writers were dead. From the vigorous generation of the twenties, only Jaroslav Seifert survived in both the literal and literary sense; and at the end of the Stalinist era, he emerged with some of the best poetry of his mature years. The second and third congresses of Czechoslovak writers brought the new literary climate into the open. The dean of Marx-Stalinist aesthetics, Ladislav Štoll, was sharply criticized and had to "confess" that his 1950 Congress speech featured the cult of the personality. The critics and writers who in 1945–48 fought for their personal positions and brazenly adopted socialist realism found themselves in a vacuum. Štoll continued to be the mouthpiece of the party, but he was no longer a feared and powerful authority. The dramatic gesture of protest came from Slovakia.

With the establishment of a fascist Slovak autonomous state in 1939, the young Slovak literature, its literary language codified only in 1851, acquired an independent status. When in 1945 the Slovaks renewed their unity with the Czechs, it was done on on terms of strict equality. The Slovak writers were proudly conscious of their independence and the Czechs respected it. For the Slovaks the war years brought an experience different from that of the Czechs: under German occupation the Czechs lost their sovereignty while the Slovaks gained theirs, even though it meant German interference with Slovak affairs. In 1942, the Slovaks went into armed resistance against the German occupants and their own totalitarian regime. Compared with the Czech underground and even with the holocaust which followed the Heydrich *attentat*, the Slovak resistance had a heroic character which found its chroniclers and poets. The post–World War II Slovak attitude has not been a separatist movement. The Slovak writer V. Mináč voices it explicitly: the coexistence of Czech and Slovaks is necessary because it benefits both sides.[3] Mináč is ready to accept the blame for some of the less noble Slovak

3. V. Mináč, *Paradoxy* (Bratislava, 1966), p. 94.

political moves and does not try to hide the fact that Slovakia had its first taste of autonomy with Hitler's "benevolence." The axis Tiso-Berlin was a defensive and protective measure. Great nations, he believes, do not abstain from certain disreputable actions if they are necessary or inevitable.[4] Czecho-Slovak relations from 1918–38 were less rosy than the Czechs wish to present them. The relationship of Czech literature toward Slovak was that of an older sister toward a younger one.[5] Now the better Slovak fiction and poetry are being translated into Czech, and some people abroad wonder whether this is not a waste of literary and economic energy, since every Czech is able to read Slovak as well as his own language; moreover, in translation the Slovak text often loses its original flavor. Nevertheless, the translations are dutifully made as a recognition of the new Czecho-Slovak mutual respect. The problem of the Slovak literary language is not linguistic but political, says the Slovak writer.[6] His essay "Tu žije národ" [Here lives a nation][7] is a happy title for the vivid discussion of the new Slovak position and its traditions handed down by L. Štúr, J. Francisci, V. P. Tóth, and S. Ormis.

Slovak self-confidence undoubtedly prompted the courageous step in the destalinization of Czechoslovak literature. Its "sensational" event was Ladislav Mňačko's *Oneskorené reportáže* [Belated reportage, 1962]. Mňačko never forgot that Slovaks fought for their liberation from both Slovak and German fascism. Whether in a novel,[8] short story, or reportage, Mňačko always reminds the reader of the virtues of the Slovak resistance which—as he sees it—should not be forgotten, lost in red tape, or corrupted by human viciousness and pettiness. *Oneskorené reportáže* is carried out in this spirit. Its leading motif is the question: čo se robí s liudmi?—how are people treated? How are

4. Ibid., pp. 86, 88.

5. Ibid., p. 93.

6. Ibid., p. 95.

7. In *Paradoxy*.

8. *Smrt sa volá Engelchen* was translated into several languages including English (*Death Is Called Engelchen* [Prague: Artia, 1961]).

those treated who offered everything they had including their own lives to the resistance movement and to the party? Like Solzhenitsyn, Mňačko wrote "for the good of the cause," though with much more urgency than the Russian author. Mňačko did not write gladly, with satisfaction or righteousness. In a way it was painful for him, but he continued because he felt it to be his duty. None should fear the truth, he said, it should be feared only when it is suppressed. He did not dress his message in fiction; he reported about real cases as a reporter or camera does. And even more important, he confessed, without trying to minimize the portent of his confession, having taken part in the public life of the Stalinist period. For him, it is not the act of repentance which matters but the present stand; in other words, it is not enough to proclaim a new cultural policy (destalinization) and make a confession at the congress (Štoll). Injustice cannot be voted on, it has to be undone.

Some of the people in *Oneskorené reportáže* still live and their plight continues. "Záhrada utrpenie" [The garden of agony] narrates the story of a political trial. People are cooperating with the prosecution, some in fear, others in good faith. The prosecutor in Mňačko's story is neither the diabolical Inquisitor nor the phantomlike inhabitant of the Castle; yet in a way he is more frightening. Before facing the Grand Inquisitor, the accused must have committed the crime, and Kafka's prosecutor does not have real dimensions. Mňačko's trial is a nightmare which everyone may dream, at least where the "crime" is ever ambiguous. Another story, "Svedok" [The witness], ostracizes the Stalinist judiciary system and its use of "confession" as the ultimate proof of guilt. To make his pleas more direct, Mňačko gives the names of Clementis and Novomeský as historical reference and adds that it is no longer easy to put an innocent man before the judge and condemn him.

It may be anyone's guess why *Oneskorené reportáže* stirred the interest of the East—it deals with the victims of the Stalinist regime and with its failures. It unveils the dishonesty of some members of the party who after the war sought lucrative positions and used any means to promote their careers (Kolajnice). The red tape harmed individual lives (Klara), the bureaucratic apparatus damaged the economy (Diár). The Western observer concluded that *Oneskorené reportáže* was an anticommunist document. He overlooked one important fact: *Oneskorené reportáže* was written by a Communist and by a party man who had no intention of hurting the party. In the 1964 introduction to *Oneskorené reportáže*, Mňačko wrote: "I am a Communist, and I love my party. . . . I wrote my book as one of its members and for the good of the party." One may ask whether this statement, especially its tone, was not written after some discussions behind closed doors—*Oneskorené reportáže* appeared first as a serial in *Kultúrný život;* however, even if some persuasion from the party's side took place, it does not retract from the importance of the book.

Mňačko was rightfully aroused when he discovered that in January 1964 *Deutsche Zeitung* published a sample of *Oneskorené reportáže* without his knowledge and when the publishing house Jacob Hegner in Cologne announced the publication of *Verbotene Reportagen* (the title was badly translated). He protested loudly, and his protest had publicity outside his country since it involved Rolf Hochhuth and his *Der Stellvertreter*. The Slovaks intended to produce the play and Hochhuth refused, giving as his reason the possible misuse of the drama for anti-Catholic propaganda. Mňačko also had reservations concerning the publication of *Oneskorené reportáže*. He addressed an open letter to Hochhuth: "I understand your apprehension about the misinterpretation of your play. . . . *Oneskorené reportáže* stirred an interest in the West. . . . I am asking you . . . what Czechoslovak literature has been published in the West up to now? Nothing—and you will not start with my book. You would be surprised if you should read the list of Western authors translated into Slovak."[9]

9. *Kultúrný život*, 1965, no. 12.

As in the 1964 introduction, Mňačko underlined his party allegiance and flatly refused to be introduced to the readers in the West as a Communist dissenter. In this he must have been sincere, although his attitude toward the publication of his work outside Czechoslovakia changed, because in March 1967 the *London Telegram* started to publish *The Taste of Power*. The Czechoslovak prepublication list announced the title *Ako chutí moc* and its Czech translation in 1966, but the book appeared only in English. Its significance, as pointed out in *Saturday Review* (19 August 1967), was historical rather than literary. Mňačko, however, is not a writer of fiction in the sense of the word as it is used in the West. For him "the writer bears responsibility for the development of his country."[10] The reviewer described the thesis of *The Taste of Power* as truism, which it is, but for Mňačko this truism is something like Cato's *ceterum autem*. His thesis treats a very special "taste for power." At the beginning its hero was a courageous partisan who did not spare himself for the good of the cause; without reproach during the resistance and revolution, he only later succumbed to power and its traps. Many others, not necessarily heads of government or dictators, were corrupted and sold their integrity or their friends to preserve their power, position, or skin. And it was because of this phenomenon of his society that Mňačko wrote the novel. Yes, it lacks what the critic has asked of it: literary sophistication, originality, so-called psychological insight. Its importance, and for that matter the importance of Mňačko's other writings, is not limited to the fictional record or the interpretation of "history"—it is not history as yet—but rests in their activist involvement in the politico-ideological struggle of contemporary Czechoslovakia. Mňačko risked more than the average dissenter: a position which every writer might envy. His exile in Israel and his

10. *Kultúrný život*, 1964, no. 30.

loss of Czechoslovak citizenship dramatize once more the situation of the contemporary Czechoslovak intellectual.[11]

Next in importance to Mňačko's criticism of the Slovak Stalinist regime is Mináč's *Záznamy* [Notes, 1963]. Mináč too pleads for justice and human dignity. The injustice to which man gave or gives his consent, whether active or passive, settles in his mind like an incurable disease. The instinct of self-preservation whispers that perhaps his friend is not so innocent and that he is right in not supporting and helping him. The corruption of the human mind extends into the field of economy: the factory has to fulfill its plan and this will be done against all odds, but on paper only. Workers, supervisors, directors, all those responsible for the production of the plan know very well that the official statement has been falsified or that the proposed norm may be fulfilled only at the cost of the quality of the product, or safety, or something else essential. Yet no one dares to dissociate himself from the false facade. Production may suffer, man may be crushed, the system has to win. A man struggles with his conscience, but his moral nausea ends in submission and he gives his yes to the falsehood. Dominik Tatarka gave the leading role to this yes in his *Démon súhlasu* [The demon of yeah]. He used the classical genre of utopian satire and eliminated the human element so urgent in Mináč's and Mňačko's stories.

The hero of *Démon súhlasu*, Bartolomej Boleraz, is an intellectual Candide in the world of the cult of the personality. The reader meets him after he has died in a plane crash while returning from a writers' conference. He has only half of his brain, the other half belongs to the comrade who traveled with him. With this satirist's gag we are introduced to the world of literary dogmatism, to the conference which had to decide on the distribution of literary Oscars. A novel about building up heavy industry and a volume of poetry with the attractive title *Tristopercent*

11. *New York Times*, 29 August 1967. See also "Všudybyl Ladislav Mňačko" in Free Europe's *Československý zpravodaj*, 1968, no. 619.

*šťastia* [Three hundred percent happiness][12] had been selected as winners. The jury and the conference members all knew that the novel was rotten and the poetry a fake; nevertheless the "demon of yeah" pushed them to vote for both. Before the session was closed, the supervisor suddenly arrived and proposed a reverse decision. Boleraz, the dissenter, had a golden opportunity to become the hero of the moment, but it was precisely the volte-face of the assembly, its collective "yeah" which paralyzed him. For him there was no point of return, the plane had to crash.

The reformist spirit of Tatarka's and Mňačko's stories also dictated *Exponent a exponáty* [Arranger and arrangements], a collection of stories by Josef Jurzet. His literary cartoons dismiss any frightening dimensions and center on the satire of the little man, the minor attendant of the committees and his private snug world. Jurzet knows how to condense into a single page, or even half a page, the caricature of a socialist bureaucrat ("Ako v rodině" [As in a family]), or of official "cultural" activities ("Pokrytec" [Hypocrite]). He exposes "criticism" and "self-criticism," as they are used in the ideo-political practice ("Oznamenie" [Announcement]) and last but not least the inefficiency of the socialist economy. ("Odborník" [Specialist].)

The Slovak literary destalinization and the second Russian "thaw" are similar in their reformist tendencies. Both *For the Good of the Cause* and *Oneskorené reportáže* cut the red tape and link economic problems with ethics, in short, point the fictional finger at the cult of the personality. Solzhenitsyn's presentation of the case is restrained and his style reminds one of classical Russian realism. Mňačko and Mináč speak a plain language; they report facts, record history, erect monuments to dead victims, and advocate justice for the living. They reiterate the meaning of the past struggle against the totalitarian oppression

12. The title has a sardonic turn directed against S. K. Neumann who in 1947 published a collection of poetry called *Sto deset procent štěstí* (Hundred and ten percent happiness).

and ask: Where are those who fought for freedom? Solzhenitsyn's criticism of the negative sides of Soviet life is balanced by the unadulterated virtues of his positive characters—the young people who give their spare time to the brigades, men who have fought in the patriotic war. Solzhenitsyn's people come from the well-known repertoire of dedicated students, teachers, and officials as opposed to "little Stalins," who are neither monsters nor villains but simply the bad grain which has to be winnowed from the good. The accusation of *For the Good of the Cause* is carried out in a sober, impartial tone, while Mňačko pleads with emotion and in an angry voice. Solzhenitsyn's protest is veiled by the surface of his narrative. The story makes it perfectly clear that the good will prevail. The crux of the offenses, the transfer of the building, is merely a technical wrong; no one is seriously hurt. Mňačko's cry "čo se robí s liudmi?" is a dramatic S. O. S. It accuses not just one deficiency, one mistake, one failure, one individual, but the whole community. Solzhenitsyn leaves no doubt that in the long run Knorozov will give place to a more efficient administrator of the national funds and resources.

Mňačko, Tatarka, and Jurzet attack more than red tape, stupidity, and accidental damage; they expose mean motivations, careerism, and personal benefits. They denounce the suppression of truth in the courtroom, which is the very place where it should shine. They are alarmed and they ring the alarm because they seem to know that evil is contagious and may destroy man's integrity. Solzhenitsyn allows a page for the discussion of the futility of some literary publication; yet he is miles away from Tatarka's Voltairian attack on literary awards. Solzhenitsyn's young people are clean-cut komsomols, their disappointment bears no trace of bitter resentment. Those youngsters cannot conceive a world where corruption might destroy the good of the cause, unless of course that world should be a capitalist world. They seem not to know about the Grand Inquisitor's office or of its impact on a people's mind.

# 13
# THE NEW ETHOS

*He knew, he knew very well that the moment would come when he would say, "I am going," and do what he had in mind. In every generation only one is able to do it, always a young man between fourteen and seventeen. . . .*

Jaroslav Putík

In comparison with the Slovak protest, the Czech voice calling for "justice" and "truth" may seem hesitant and conformist at first. The man for whom it speaks has all the qualifications of a good party man: he was in the concentration camp or took part in the resistance movement and was known as a shock-worker. Accused of political crimes, he is unable to see his guilt and make the necessary "confession." So far the Czech and the Slovak version agree. But as the trial goes on the accused himself discovers that he has been blinded by self-deception and that he *is* guilty. This turn, which in the Slovak story was the result of coercive measures, in the Czech story[1] brings about a catharsis: although the man is expelled from the party—three months of imprisonment are his penalty, a light punishment indeed—he will be given the opportunity to start at the bottom as a common worker, his Communist faith unimpaired. The message is strictly orthodox: never relax in your vigilance to adjust your individual views to those of the party.

Many other stories published around the year 1960 arrived at

1. Lenka Hašková, *Obžalovaný* (Prague, 1960).

a similar conclusion. Two or three years later, such a regular message was outdated and its sanctimonious clichés replaced by refreshing directness: ". . . tak sakra, budujeme socialismus pro lidi nebo pro pravdu . . ." (damn it, do we build socialism for the people's sake or for the truth's sake).[2] This new voice and its tone belong to the generation tired of "heroism," tired also of optimism and its Marxist phraseology; it is allergic to any sign of pretense or dishonesty. The German occupation sensitized its moral consciousness. It was then that they learned the real meaning of such words as betrayal, hunger, torture, lie, love. The less-talented writers still depend on the socialist-realist formula, its brigades, building-construction projects, and Marxist ethics of the communal life. Yet, whether one reads about the industrial production or people in love, the foremost value seems to be the integrity of human existence. In the novel *Přesýpací hodiny* [The hourglass],[3] a Communist journalist writes successfully about brigades, the aims of revolution, and the goals of the socialist way of life. In his zeal he does not notice that his originally honest intentions have become routine and that he is producing stilted clichés, which alienate him from his closest friends and eventually are rejected by the party itself. The moral of the story? "What was successful in the fifties has no chance for success today, this you must know."[4] The sixties signal a turn from the socialist-realist varnish—Russians and Czechs have a good expression for it: *lakirovka* and *lakýrovka*, respectively.

A novel often discussed in Czechoslovakia, which has none of this varnish, is *Páteř* [The spine] by Ladislav Bublík.[5] Written in the rugged slang of the people working at the construction of an industrial compound near Moravská Ostrava, it protests corruption, lies, and opportunism. The community contains villains who use the party as a screen for their meanness; but it also has men who try to live honestly and without false pretensions. A

2. Jan Trefulka, *Pršelo jim štěstí* (Prague, 1963), p. 103.

3. Karel Houba, *Přesýpací hodiny* (Prague, 1964).

4. Ibid., p. 128.

5. (Moravská Ostrava, 1963.)

decade or so ago, Marie Pujmanová's brigades of young men and women glowed with optimism and smiled toward the bright future. During a short ten-year period those promising pioneers were corrupted (*zlajdačili*). From Pujmanová's youth one heard a nonchalant, sporty, sometimes affected slang. People in *Páteř* speak a vivacious language mixed with the dialect of the region and spiced with German and Russian words. The narrator of *Páteř* tells us that he and his characters were raised on class hatred—that same hatred of which Orwell wrote so imaginatively; he concedes that in the past such hatred has perhaps been justified, since it helped to cement the proletarians. Now it has become a malignancy which may spread in the group by which it is practiced, the proletarians themselves. Should a man surrounded by the morally sick fight for his integrity and eventually die for it, or should he give in and admit his defeat? The answer contains an objection: If we shall be judged because we kept silent, we will be judged rightfully; but were we not gagged and did they not put on us the straitjacket of fear? "It was in the fifties, you must remember, something was in the air, fear, yes, it was fear. There was war in Korea and here people were being arrested, it all had its own logic. . . ."[6]

The Czech literature of the sixties continues to bring out situations in which the accused man, the suspected man, or simply the nonconformist is on trial. With some writers the touch is light, the pressure bearable. Even such ominous words as security measures (*prověření*) and clearance (*kádrování*) are pronounced with irony. It could be that some of those authors would refuse to be called moralists. Yet what else is the compulsion which prompts them to expose profitable operations in private and public life and to examine the pressures around and in them?

In this literary community one group distinguishes itself by its new language and its irreverence for the established values. The authors of this group are antiromantic—this is their defense against sentiment, an obvious luxury in the present hard-

6. Jaroslav Putík, *Smrtelná neděle* (Prague, 1967), p. 71.

ship of life—and all have a strong sense of humor. They look back on Hašek and Čapek, though with some reservations.[7] If asked which of the foreign authors they read, they might give the names of Bellow or Cayrol, Sarraute, or Robbe-Grillet.[8] One of this antiromantic group is Jan Trefulka, quoted earlier. In one of his stories, the following stanza is sung by an artist who makes propaganda posters:

*Až náš proletariát*
*zdrtí kapitalistickej řád*
*pak přijdou ty krásný chvílée*
*o kerejch psal Marx ve svým dílée.*

("When our proletarian mass / will crush the capitalist class / then those blessed moments will arrive / which Karl Marx so well described.")[9] The translation, however, cannot convey, the enjoyable flavor these words have in the native land of the good soldier Schweik. The lackadaisical tone has sharp edges: ". . . and the next year the beetroots will freeze in the ground once more."[10] Programming, competitions, new policies—they all end in a lifeless absurdity. Normalcy can and will prevail only when everyone works honestly without slogans and their protective *lakirovka.* Trefulka's man is eager to speak out, yet all he is allowed to say is yes. If some one is praised, he has to join the praise; if some one is thrown out of the party or work, he has to vote yes exactly like the hero of Tatarka's "Demon of Yeah." The Czechoslovak writer should not seek an alibi in "history" or hide behind the current slogans; let him confess "what he did and *was not forced to do* [italics mine] . . . how many times he compromised with his own conscience, how often he shirked his responsibility . . . all this must be counted and accounted for, and only then let him talk about heroism." The quotation is

7. Jiří Robert, *Hovory s veverkou* (Prague, 1963), p. 65.

8. *Nové knihy*, 1966, no. 19.

9. Trefulka, *Třiatřicet stříbrných křepelek* (Prague, 1965), p. 22.

10. Ibid., p. 33.

from a collective publication[11] and was written by Jaroslav Putík, another of the nonconformist authors. In one of his stories we encounter once more the man summoned by the court ("Pozvání k soudu");[12] the man goes through stages of the monstrous fear of one who is not guilty and yet is afraid that he will be sentenced. When after the agony of apprehension he presents himself at the court, he learns that the trial has been postponed and will take place only in ten years. This anticlimax is not a flight into the absurd; it is a mere shift in dimension, a moralistic turn.

Less "absurd" is the case of a man, in "Milosrdná sestra" [Sister of charity], sentenced to ten years in prison because he has let an old friend stay overnight in his house, not knowing that he intends to cross the border illegally. By the complete innocence of the accused, the author made his case unequivocal. Let us suppose that his man knew about the friend's intention; was it his duty to refuse him shelter and to inform the police? Putík did not press his hero into such a crucial decision; he tested him again, another time. He was visited by the devil (in the story "Před svítáním přišel ke mně ďábel"), who whispered to him not to protest the wrongs he had witnessed. If you do so, the devil told him, you will be waking up at dawn as you have been lately and you will have no rest. Forget all this mess which is no concern of yours and sleep peacefully. Such a happy creature ("Hodný člověk"), minding his own business, is the Czechoslovak citizen of the sixties. He has all the reason to be contented: he was able to save money and buy himself a Spartak (a Czech Chevrolet), he drives well and enjoys driving, his fellowmen consider him to be a law-abiding colleague. In short, he has nothing to fear, and yet is not at peace within himself. He does not seem quite healthy and "positive." He feels guilty and has an irresistible urge to agree with others even before they express their opinions. Together with this mental twist, he has a strong drive

11. *Pro a proti,* Kritická ročenka, 1963 (Prague, 1964), p. 88.

12. From the collection of short stories bearing the same title (as are the other Putík stories mentioned).

to be bad; he yearns for pain, for a good, clean-cut pain to replace his regular communal happiness.

> Sometimes I recall with nostalgia an irretrievable past. By this I mean the Erinys. They remind me of women who complain to the shopkeeper that they were sold bad eggs and do not stop until justice is done to them. Moreover, I do not see why the goddesses of wrathful revenge should be described as hideous. I myself never saw a man staunchly defending justice who appeared ugly to me. Only a person who is afraid of possible Erinys and has a bad conscience may see them with snakes in their hair and with claws instead of hands; with these the Erinys are supposed to tear at the back of their victim's neck; they chase them all over the world, yelling frightfully.
>
> However, beautiful or not, those adamantine Erinys sleep their eternal dream in the kingdom of Hades.
>
> No one is afraid of them any more.
>
> Eichmann killed six million people; he loved canaries and was a good sleeper.
>
> Murderers are often good sleepers.
>
> Bad conscience may be treated in a pleasant way by taking a health-vacation in the mountains.
>
> Also books teaching that evil is not quite as bad as one may think, if it eventually results in some good, brings peace to a disturbed mind.
>
> Anguish is successfully healed by psychiatrists and certain drugs [*guajacuran*].
>
> For headaches aspirin [*algena*] suffices.[13]

Moralities often used classical allegory. Yet the above quotation is more then a sample of current Czech literature; it covers the contemporary moral code of the nation. Its allegory is clear to everyone: the ethics of man suffered a mortal blow. Wholesale criminals were at large as respected members of human society. They had tender feelings for their pets, and if a neighbor complained that he lost his sleep by witnessing evil, he got the answer: you are oversensitive, my friend; we cannot be bothered by individual cases, it is the final good which sanctifies our means.

The generation which lived during the period of such policies

13. Putík, *Indicie* (Prague, 1963), p. 23.

took part in the 1945–48 revolution, and came to full maturity in the sixties, felt it necessary to examine its own conscience. In the short story "Řeč nad hrobem" [The funeral speech][14] the class members of 1945, gathered around the grave of a classmate, realize that something has been lost since their commencement day. In between, many of them learned how to lie to others and to themselves and to accept the compromise of profitable situations. In comparison with Mňačko's direct and frontal attack on the facade of justice and public morals, the touch of "Řeč nad hrobem" is light, discreet, tempered by fiction; yet it is no less eloquent. The present code of ethics is relentlessly questioned and examined whether in the sophisticated *Jeronym na pouti*,[15] first novel of Petr Pujman, son of Marie Pujmanová, or in *Hrdina pátek*,[16] by Eduard Petiška.

After the relativism of the two world wars and after the shock of totalitarian regimes, the ethical issues appear again both in fictional and theoretical writings. *Morálka dnes a zajtra* [Morals of today and tomorrow][17] is a collective publication proposing social relations in which man would treat his fellow man like a brother. The most articulate member of this group is Milan Machovec. His book *Smysl lidského života* [Sense of human life][18] is significantly introduced by two mottos, one by Marx, the other by Teilhard de Chardin. It is of course the latter's *Le phénomène humain* and not *Le milieu divin* that the Czech author has in mind. Machovec takes it for granted that modern man is incapable of religious faith. However, he indicts him because "he does not know how to die."[19] As a remedy, Machovec proposes

14. Ludmila Romportlová, *Papoušek zmizel* (Prague, 1962), pp. 93–98.

15. Petr Pujman, *Jeronym na pouti* [Jerome's journey] (Prague, 1968).

16. Eduard Petiška, *Hrdina pátek* [The hero Friday] (Prague, 1968).

17. Jiří Jánský, Milan Machovec, and Martin Marušiák, *Morálka dnes a zajtra* (Bratislava, 1962).

18. Milan Machovec, *Smysl lidského života* (Prague, 1965).

19. Ibid., pp. 23, 228.

a positivist humanism based on the continuity of life in one's child, in one's family, and in its extension, the human race. It is at this point that the Czechoslovak philosopher and writer see eye to eye. *Rozhovory bez konca* [Discussions without end] by Dominik Tatarka expresses the same idea—that biological transcendency is the redeeming element of individual life. Tatarka's first-person narrator, when faced with death during World War II, thinks about his mother and sister; he prays "not to the powers of heaven but to his mother and to his children's mother."[20] This brings us back to the positivist (not the Teilhardian) belief in the transcendency of matter and to its ensuing moral attitudes; it seems that in the long run man is unable to wave aside the transcendental perspective.

20. Dominik Tatarka, *Rozhovory bez konca* (Bratislava, 1965), p. 193.

# 14
# UNMISTAKABLY DIFFERENT

WHEN THE book *Zbabělci* [Cowards] by J. Škvorecký appeared in 1959, it acted like an explosive on the outwardly smooth surface of Czech literary production. Unlike the proper novels about the German occupation and the underground of World War II, it treated the Czech history of May 1945 with little respect. Moreover, the attitude expressed in *Zbabělci* toward values of life in general was offbeat. As if unaware of his responsibilities toward society, the youthful hero of *Zbabělci* displayed a love for jazz—his escape from the nightmare of the German occupation—and although he took the right stand in the May uprising—he went to greet the Russian army—he was not disposed to listen to the high-sounding speeches delivered for the benefit of the populace. The vivid flow of Škvorecký's prose had the effect of a fresh breeze entering a room which had not been aired for years. Abroad the reaction was strong. Czech exiles thought *Zbabělci* a great literary event, and the Western analyst discerned in it a sign of revolt. Both were wrong. True, Škvorecký's book was retired from the market and made available again only after the destalinization of Czechoslovak censorship, but when its second edition was published it was already evident that *Zbabělci* was merely a harbinger of a new literary climate and not the leader of "political" opposition to the regime; it was also obvious that, though he was the first, Škvorecký was by no means the only talent of the present generation. Still, his *Zbabělci* remained an issue since it denounced cowardice that poses as heroism.[1]

Škvorecký wrote the novel when he was twenty-four and close to the age of his hero, Dany Smiřický; the book, considered to be an attack on any kind of cliché and dissimulation, had to wait twenty-one years for legitimate publication. Škvorecký is quite open about his likes and dislikes; he admires Armstrong and jazz and he has read quite a few American authors,[2] who in his view have something in common with the contemporary directions of Czech prose and poetry. But it is not the American book-of-the-month which interests the Czech intellectual; he prefers Ferlinghetti and his "unfair arguments with existence." The authors of the sixties are coming back to the cosmopolite tradition of modern Czech literature; they are conscious of their sweeping turn from the objective narrative, whether its subject be history or socialism; they underline the veracity of the writer's experience, which in their literary practice means: if by chance you decide to write about construction works, let it be a part of your experience and not a "political" choice. Unlike most literary innovators, some of the new Czech authors are extremely popular. The short stories by Bohumil Hrabal, for example, are in great demand by such periodicals as *Mladá fronta*, *Naše vojsko*, *Smena*, and *Svět Sovětů*.

Born in 1914, Bohumil Hrabal is one of the authors who dominate the contemporary Czech literary scene. In 1967 the film based on Hrabal's *Ostře sledované vlaky* (*Closely Watched Trains*) received the Grand Prix at the international festival in Mann-

1. *Pro a proti*, Kritická ročenka, 1964 (Prague, 1965), pp. 88, 89.

2. Ibid., p. 42; see also his *Nápady čtenáře detektivek* [Comments of a reader of mystery stories] (Prague, 1965), in which Škvorecký shows how well he is acquainted with American authors such as Dashiell Hammett and Raymond Chandler.

heim, West Germany. *Ostře sledované vlaky* is noteworthy because the story takes place during the German occupation of Czechoslovakia and yet it is free of the patriotic-ideological elements usually found in resistance fiction. The "heroic" deed—a bomb thrown at a German train—is merely a dramatic climax in the life of an adolescent. His action is as directly and sincerely motivated as is his effort to get rid of his virginity. Hrabal's stories glorify the force of life whether on the auto racetrack ("Smrt pana Batisberga") or in an adolescent love. Death's shadow is a mere complement to the body of life. Hrabal delights in the stumbling blocks of human existence which, seen from the outside, release laughter. Yet deep down, behind the "joke" and its often obscene words describing the so-called facts of life, there exists a tender sentiment even though it never rises to the surface. This tenderness is due to a love for life and an affection for those who live it without crutches.

The reasons which prevented Hrabal from publishing before the literary thaw are evident. His *Taneční hodiny pro starší a pokročilé* [Advanced dancing classes for the elderly], written in 1946, had to wait for publication until 1964, but since then has had several editions. This story, a tour de force, is written in one single sentence from beginning to end. It was translated into Polish and French, and its most remarkable success was the German edition published by Suhrkamp. His *Inzerát na dům, ve kterém už nechci bydlet* [An ad to sell the house where I do not want to live anymore] touches upon problems treated in another form by Mňačko or Putík—the falsity and lies in public and private life. With Hrabal, morality has an "absurd" twist. In the story "Divní lidé," Hrabal describes a scene parallel to one in *Oneskorené reportáže:* journalists visit an industrial plant to gather material for a propaganda film. But where Mňačko records only relevant facts—the varnish of propaganda—Hrabal lights up some seemingly irrelevant detail: the supervisor of the forced-labor team cuts out an angel painted on a child's bed which has been discarded on a heap of rubbish. Although Hrabal refuses to chant the slogans proposed by the party, he speaks with irony about the Czechs in exile and about Radio Free Europe.[3] This is hardly a political gesture; for him such people are pictures from old magazine issues.

The group of new authors unwilling to compromise "successfully" with socialist realism, though not homogeneous, share in a protest against the dehumanized world where man is forced to live "zprostředkovaně" (by proxy). The language of this generation is entirely devoid of ornamental tropes; its indifference toward the past is amazing and spreads to the readers. An article in the publisher's magazine *Nové knihy*, advertizing a particular book, stressed that it was worthy of interest in spite of being "koncentráčnická literatura" (concentration camp literature). The writer of those lines did not, because he could not, mean anything offensive since he was writing for a publisher's magazine; yet he expressed the fact that the public is tired of literature exploiting the past. "Art is not obligatory" (*umění je nepovinné*); it cannot be reduced to any literary theory and made to order. The period of "dogmatism," when monuments were built of stones as well as words, is over.[4] The reference is clear: "monuments" of stone must be the monumental statue of Stalin which dominated the view of Prague and which has been removed. "Monuments in words" may refer to Nezval's verse (or that of any other poet) written in praise and honor of the cult of the personality. "Monuments" may also signify the memoirs and chronicles of the past "socialist struggle," novels with subjects from the history of socialism such as those of the late president Antonín's Zápotocký[5]—*Vstanou noví bojovníci* (1948), or *Rudá záře and Kladnem* (1951). *Kritická ročenka* did not hesitate to call them and their like the "catastrophes of Czech fiction."

Also symptomatic of the present franchise in literary affairs is the comment of the periodical *Plamen*,[6] which reported that

3. *Inzerát na dům, ve kterém už nechci bydlet* (Prague, 1965), pp. 47–49.

4. *Pro a proti*, Kritická ročenka, 1964, p. 47.

5. Antonín Zápotocký (1884–1957) was premier from 1948 to 1952, and president from 1953 to 1957.

6. *Plamen*, 1964, no. 1, p. 60.

the verses in honor of the arrival of President Beneš at Prague in 1945 were omitted in the new editions of Seifert and Hora. *Plamen* of course had no intention of rehabilitating President Beneš's memory, nor did it mean to touch upon Seifert's and Hora's ideological past; it was simply a protest against politico-ideological manipulations in the realm of literature. Let the writer stand for his work, let him be tried on his own grounds. Literature is what it has never ceased to be: an instance of human condition for which the author and his work must answer, both now and in the future.

Although the Czechoslovak writer has started his campaign for freedom on literary grounds, his effort—if it is really concerned with the integrity of man and his society as he claims—must surely bring him to a more general point of view. Thus in every situation, whether literary or economic, he is confronting the system in power with the reality of "life around him." Let the clichés disappear not merely from the novel but also from the economic report. The fourth Congress of Czechoslovak Writers in June 1967 brought those issues into focus; it was an event which sparked the political-ideological crisis inside Czechoslovakia. The discussions rehashed the well-known, ready-made phrases about socialist freedom, responsibility, humanity, people, nation, democracy, revolution, and reaction—phrases characteristic of a public platform that is not necessarily in Czechoslovakia. After the dust of words settled down, it was clear that the party was determined to maintain its literary dictatorship and that some of the writers were equally determined to oppose it.

Still, the manifesto of Czechoslovak writers as it was released in London and published in the United States seems to be forged.[7] Its language is simply not that of the Czechoslovak dissenters. Its "false" tone is obvious, especially when compared with the genuine reports and speeches at the congress, one of which reached the West through private channels. One recog-

7. Pavel Kohout read it first in Hamburg in the Sunday *Times*. *Literární listy*, 28 February 1968.

nizes not only the author but also the tenor of the current Czechoslovak protest: "the Czechoslovak writers decided to meet, but before they made this decision they had to get the permission to decide. . . ." The speech also voiced the questions recurrent in Czechoslovak fiction: Why were the rehabilitated people not reinstated with their full civil rights? Why were their former apartments not returned to them? The voice heard at the congress spoke for the man whose life and work were wrecked by the policies of the Stalinist era, who was ostracized by a society which he had helped build with youthful enthusiasm, who read poetry written by Halas and Novomeský, like himself, accused of deviation.

After 1965 the poets were allowed to publish again and the excommunicated persons were able to return to their work and public life. But some things could not be restituted or compensated. It was not just the time spent in prison or under less spectacular punishments; they had lost confidence in their fellow men. The hero of Kundera's novel[8] used to ask himself the following question: "Would this man or woman on whom I am looking right now vote 'yes' or 'no' on my expulsion from the party?" No one should try to answer such a question, said the writer speaking at the congress, and even if he dared to do so, his answer would not reach the public. It never did. The opposition had to be crushed or at least strongly discouraged. The writers, Ludvík Vaculík, Ivan Klíma, Antonín Liehm, were expelled from the party; Jan Procházka had to leave the Central Committee. *Literární noviny*, the hive of dissent, changed hands; its staff was reshuffled and later also its title—instead of *Literární noviny* it was *Literární listy*, although in daily communications it made little difference, since now as before it is called *Literárky*. Mňačko was the only Slovak who attended the Prague congress. The Slovak writers had their own conference in September 1967. Dominik Tatarka resigned; Laco Novomeský on the other hand, accepted his election.

Not all the outstanding Czechoslovak writers were involved in

8. Milan Kundera, *Žert* (Prague, 1967).

the dispute. Some prominent names did not appear either on the punitive or the promotion list. Art and music were left untouched. Literature only, this Muse whom the Marxists dethroned from her lofty pedestal, to whom they assigned the duty of attending meetings and working for the propaganda, only she suffered because she asked for some antisocial privileges and defended the "European" character of the Czechoslovak socialist revolution against the "satellite" politico-literary concept.[9] The party knew very well that it could not do entirely without her; it knew, however, that at any time it might enforce its power and that it would always find some professionals to comply to its will. The party also learned that this is not the desired state of affairs or a permanent solution of the tensions between its rule and the Muse in question.

Since then, the dialogue between the militant Czechoslovak intellectual and his public on one side, and the party on the other, has continued unremittingly, its most articulate protagonists speaking from the platform of *Literární listy.* For months the outcome of the dialogue remained dubious, although one issue was clear: the "May generation of 1968" stepped forward with vigor reminiscent of the historic "May generation of 1858"; they both had the courage to demand freedom not merely for their literary domain but for the whole nation; like the poets and writers of 1858, those fighters of 1968 aspired to be an integral part of their European heritage, its traditions, and values.

In 1968, more urgently then ever, the Czechoslovak intellectual pleaded for his nation—videant consules ne quid res publica detrimenti capiat—but his effort to free it from the role of a satellite was supressed with brutal force. Once more the Czechs could quote Halas's line lamenting the betrayal of Czechoslovakia in 1938: "a my jsme vás milovali . . ." (and we were in love with you).[10] In the past, "you" meant the West; thirty years later it could be addressed to the once "beloved" Russia.

9. *Literární noviny,* 15 September 1967.

10. From his poem *Zpěv úzkosti* in *Torso naděje.*

## ACKNOWLEDGMENTS

I wish to express my appreciation and gratitude to my friend Eleanor D. Towle who selflessly and helpfully assisted me in editing the manuscript.

# INDEX OF NAMES

PG 5002.5 .R8 S6

Sou ckov a, Milada, 1899-
1983.

A literary satellite